*For Evie, Tajae, Tavia
and Tess*

Table of Contents

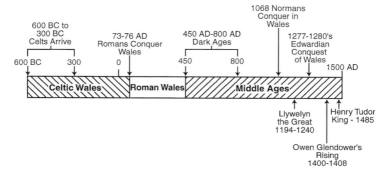

Early Welsh History

600 BC to 300 BC Celts Arrive

73-76 AD Romans Conquer Wales

450 AD-800 AD Dark Ages

1068 Normans Conquer in Wales

1277-1280's Edwardian Conquest of Wales

600 BC   300   0   450   800   1500 AD

Celtic Wales   Roman Wales   Middle Ages

Llywelyn the Great 1194-1240

Henry Tudor King - 1485

Owen Glendower's Rising 1400-1408

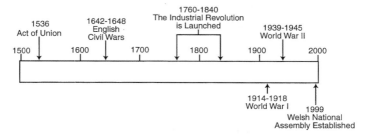

Wales in Recent Centuries

1536 Act of Union

1642-1648 English Civil Wars

1760-1840 The Industrial Revolution is Launched

1939-1945 World War II

1500   1600   1700   1800   1900   2000

1914-1918 World War I

1999 Welsh National Assembly Established

Timeline of Welsh history.

Introduction

Many books have been written about Wales and the Welsh. Most have been by Welsh people with either a Welsh or British audience in mind. Americans are likely to find such studies difficult or frustrating because there are so many references and allusions familiar to a British readership that remain vague or unknown to most Americans. *Wales: An Illustrated History* is a book primarily for a non-Welsh readership, whether they are Americans or people of other nationalities. It is designed to be useful for persons planning a trip to Wales or for students who wish to study in Wales or gain background for the study of some Welsh topic.

While Wales has fewer than three million inhabitants in an area just about the size of New Jersey, it has sent emigrants out in all directions since the Middle Ages. Millions of Americans are descended from Welsh immigrants and this book is written for them also. It is also for those readers who, for whatever reasons, have always been curious about how Wales' got to be what it is but were unwilling to bury themselves in a long and complicated study. Perhaps some of these readers may be English, because Welsh history is often given scant treatment in England.

The following pages contain a brief and basic history of this small, beautiful and romantic country from the earliest times to the present. Since Welsh history is complex, every effort has been made to present the main factors and lines of development, as well as the major personalities who have appeared on the stage of Welsh history.

Welsh history has generated a strong and controversial nationalism among many Welsh people. This book strives to present a balanced, unbiased account. Certain aspects of contemporary Wales that are often topics of debate, such as the economy, problems of society and the ongoing struggle to preserve Welsh culture have been given special treatment in the last sections of the book.

This is a book by an American author with no Welsh ancestry who has visited Wales many times, always with great enjoyment. Since the Welsh language will be an eternal mystery for the author, names and terms have been anglicized, with apologies, as they are in most other books for English speakers.

The Geographic, Ethnic and Political Setting

Wales is a small, beautiful part of the island of Britain. It is in the form of a rectangular shaped peninsula with a big bite taken out in the middle, called Cardigan Bay. The bite gives the big peninsula two smaller peninsulas of its own, Pembroke peninsula in the south and Lleyn peninsula in the north.

Wales is a very small entity. All of Wales comprises only 8,019 square miles, which is just about the size of either New Jersey or Massachusetts. Colorado is almost thirteen times larger than Wales and the State of New York is almost seven times as large. Wales measures only 130 miles from the northern coast to the southern and only 40 miles from east to west at the narrowest point. No place in Wales is more than 50 miles from the sea.

The Welsh are spread across a lovely land of generally poor soil and rugged terrain. Blue hills, dark mountains, gem-like small towns and golden or mudflat beaches are found throughout north and central Wales. In south Wales, a conurbation runs along the southern coast of the region. Cardiff, the capital of Wales and several other cities are located along this strip, which used to be within one of the world's greatest coal mining and steel making centers. The scars and ugliness from massive industrialization in this part of Wales have been lessened in recent

Wales' Neighbors

Norway

North Sea

Scotland

Ireland

Irish Sea

Wales

England

Netherlands

Cornwall

Belgium

English Channel

France

Brittany

Historic Celtic regions
where some Celtic language
is maintained

decades. Now the mines are silent and grass now grows on the slag heaps, which are called "tips" in Britain.

The effect of the Atlantic Ocean on the climate of Wales is paramount. The ocean cools the province in the summer, warms it in the winter and keeps it wet and chilly all the year round. Were it not for the warm flow of the Gulf Stream bringing water up from the south, Wales might have a climate similar to Labrador, Canada, which actually occupies the same latitude as the British Isles.

Wales is one of the very wettest parts of Europe. Prevailing southwesterly winds lift clouds of moisture out of the Atlantic low-pressure areas to drench Wales perpetually, guaranteeing a cool, moist climate in all seasons. Plants thrive but people can become depressed by skies containing so much moisture and grayness. Fortunately, nearly all of the rain that comes down in Wales takes the form of drizzle, mist and gentle downpours rather than storms. Clouds and dampness are normal, while bright, sunny days are exceptional and treasured.

England to the east receives considerably less rainfall because the high, rough country of Wales catches some of this incoming Atlantic moisture. Average rainfall amounts clearly reveal this situation: Wales gains 60 inches per year; the southern and eastern lowlands of England only 30 inches, similar to rainfall in the eastern United States. Many parts of the western United States receive only fifteen inches of rain or less. Over the years, Wales has set records for rainfall in the British Isles.

As a result of this rainfall, much of Wales is waterlogged. There are perpetual wetlands, and some bogs and rivers seem to be everywhere. Five major rivers run southward and two flow northward and two flow westward. Over 500 lakes are scattered throughout the principality.

Most of the topography of Wales is rugged and rocky. Four-fifths of Wales is made up of what is called "hard upland," where the soil is thin and rocky and only sheep and goats can make the most of the terrain. There are some soft valleys along the edges of Wales, particularly in the south, and here lowland farming has been carried on for centuries. Yet the mountains and hills predominate, including the highest peak in Britain, Snowdonia at 3,560 feet.

All the dangerous wild animals that once roamed the mountains and forests, including wolves and wildcats, are gone. They have been replaced by sheep, which far outnumber people in Wales. There are also many domestic goats and some clusters of wild goats in remote areas. At one time much of south Wales was covered by thick natural forests. Industrialization caused deforestation because timber was used for mining construction and wood was turned into charcoal for early iron smelting. In recent years, massive commercial timber planting has proceeded in many parts of Wales, creating fast-growing, uniform human-made forests containing very few different species of trees.

The Welsh are just one of three nationalities on the island of Britain. The Scots, the English and the Welsh can all safely be called "British," a term which refers to anyone living on the island. Yet, it is a very grave mistake for a foreign visitor to call either a Welsh or a Scots person "English." The three nationalities, plus Northern Ireland, are constitutionally united and comprise the

The highest peak in Britain, Snowdonia stands at 3,560 feet.

"United Kingdom." Wales is a principality of the United Kingdom, but that is merely a ceremonial title. Wales may be a nation or a country in the eyes of many, but it is not a sovereign state and it is not separated from the United Kingdom. It has its own Assembly now, as part of a new federal-style arrangement called devolution, plus its own capital, Cardiff. It has its own distinctive postage stamps but not its own currency. Wales has a striking green, white and red dragon flag, but Britain's Union Jack always represents Wales overseas.

The name Wales comes from an ancient Anglo-Saxon designation of the Welsh as foreigners. Their word for foreigner was "Wealas." The Welsh name for Wales is *Cymru*. The Welsh people are *Y Cymry*, and the Welsh language is *Cymraeg*. The medieval Latin name for Wales was Cambria and it gave rise to the English adjective Cambrian, which means pertaining to Wales. English speakers have always found it easier to anglicize Welsh names, and this practice is followed throughout these pages.

Of the three nationalities, the English predominate overwhelmingly in numbers and take up most of the space in Britain. England is over six times as large as Wales and has over 47 million people as well as most of the economic power and wealth of Britain. Wales has only just over 2.8 million people. Scotland is almost four times as large as Wales and has over five million people. Recent tabulations of ethnicity in Britain put the English at 81.5 percent, Scottish, 9.6 percent, Irish, 2.4 percent, and Welsh, 1.9 percent. The small percentage remaining beyond these four ethnic groups are from all over the rest of the world.

Flowers in bloom in downtown Swansea in January. The warm Gulf Stream keeps Wales surprisingly warm and unsurprisingly wet in the winter.

A large number of people in Wales are not Welsh in origin. Many English people have settled thickly in the southeast and northeast from the times of the Industrial Revolution. More recently they have come to live in Wales as retirees and business professionals. Large numbers of poor Irish arrived in the 19th century, and Scots came in some numbers to work for English operations in Wales. In the 20th century, immigrants of various ethnicities came from assorted parts of the collapsing British Empire. Meanwhile, Welsh emigrants have clustered in London, Liverpool, Scranton, Pennsylvania, and a hundred other places around the globe.

Wales Before the Celts

The earliest millennia of humankind in Wales are dim to us now. Very little is known about the Old and New Stone Ages, the Bronze Age and the early Iron Age. During the Stone Age, the thinnest of populations of hunter-gatherers struggled for existence in cold, wet Wales. They used primitive weapons to hunt small and large wild animals, including reindeer, and also fished in lakes and streams and gleaned food at the seashore.

Unlike the early people of the Stone Age in France and Spain, those in Wales did not leave any beautiful cave art. What was left in Wales were the remains of stone villages and turf covered hill forts as well as strange circles of boulders, burial chambers marked with great cairn stones and odd, isolated boulders that may have been boundary markers or memorials. People living centuries later would treat these remnants suspiciously and endow them with special powers for either good or evil.

Farming began in the New Stone Age, around 4,000 B.C. Apparently farming allowed an increase in numbers causing competition for good land. There is evidence that society became more warlike because hundreds of hill forts were built. Undoubtedly, these Stone Age farmers and warriors were grouped into tribes that formed shifting, violent confederations.

Sunrise from Snowdonia.
COURTESY OF THE WALES TOURIST BOARD.

The Prehistoric Celts —
600 B.C. to 73 A.D.

The Celtic heritage is of fundamental and enduring importance to the Welsh. (Celtic, by the way, is pronounced with a "k" sound rather than the "s" sound used by the famous Boston basketball team.) This heritage sets them apart from the English, who are not Celtic. The English are largely descendants of the great flood of Germanic barbarians called the Anglo-Saxons who swamped the people living on the eastern plains of Britain in the 5th to the 7th centuries A.D. The Welsh, by contrast, have always been able to trace their ancestry to the Celts, who arrived first. For a time, the Celtic tribes flourished all over the island of Britain and were known to the world as the Britons. Once the Anglo-Saxons stormed the island, the Celts to the east of Wales were overwhelmed by them. In Wales the Celts continued to remain unconquered and receive Celtic refugees from the English conquest. This historical and ethnic circumstance is the very basis of the proposition that Wales has always been a separate nation from the England of the Anglo-Saxons.

Wales is not alone as a Celtic nation with pride in its own Celtic language. The Irish, the Scots, the Cornish of Cornwall and the Bretons of France all have a Celtic heritage. It is most clearly expressed in what remains of the old folk languages. The Welsh, Irish, Scots Gaelic, Cornish and Breton languages all belong to the same family, just as French, Spanish and Italian all belong to the family of romance languages. Celtic languages diverged early, and linguists are intensely preoccupied with differences in early usage that are extremely confusing to non-professionals.

Before the advance of the Roman Empire, Iron Age Celtic peoples dominated the parts of Europe where contemporary France, Spain, Switzerland, Belgium, Britain and Ireland exist. In struggles lasting several centuries, the civilized Romans and the uncivilized German tribes drove them out of the best lands.

Who were the Celts? This is one of the more mysterious historical questions that has been long and vigorously debated by historians. Clearly identifying them among other prehistoric peoples is a major problem. Many scholars identify them by language, others by physical remains (especially those of a style named *La Tene*), and others rely upon classical Roman sources describing Celts in central and western Europe.

Varying dates are given for the arrival of the first Celts in Wales. Perhaps the first visitors reached the south coasts of the island of Britain by 1000 B.C., or 600 B.C., a more commonly cited date, or even later, 500 B.C. What is more certain is that the roots of a distinctive Celtic Welsh culture in lowland villages can be detected spreading over the centuries dating from 300 to 100 B.C. Many Celtic hill forts were erected on the west coast and in the southwestern area of Wales.

The early Celts in Wales carried on a pastoral economy, valuing cattle in particular, but also tilling the soil to grow crops of wheat, barley and flax on small fields. While their settlements were crude, their decorations of weapons, pottery and ornaments did display a remarkable artistry.

Undoubtedly the Celts dominated the people who had settled in Wales before them and gradually amalgamated with them. This Celtic supremacy in Wales existed for six or seven hundred years before the Romans subdued them. During this long stretch of history, Celtic culture evolved and so strongly rooted itself that contemporary Wales remains strongly influenced by its Celtic heritage in many ways.

Celtic Wales was fragmented politically but culturally unified. Tribes based on extended families raided neighbors for cattle and horses and fought petty wars, often in alliances that could form and dissolve rapidly. Although they called some leaders kings, they were actually tribal chieftains. Despite their constant divisions, Celts in Wales did have a common language, technology, economy and way of life. They were noted for their skills in using iron and for living in fortified hilltop settlements. Classical Roman authors described Celtic warriors with tall helmets, their bodies painted with a blue dye called woad and their hair thickened with a lime wash. These formidable warriors preferred to fight from war chariots and accompanied by dogs.

Celtic culture was conveyed in a treasured language. Bards and poets were always held in high esteem. Chieftains had a retinue of bards who were rigorously trained to memorize vast amounts of information, especially tales of gods, goddesses, heroes and heroines. These stories were passed on in this manner from generation to generation until the times of Christianity, when scribes and monks wrote many of them down. While these stories eventually received a Christian gloss from the churchmen, much of their ancient, pagan content was carried over by the monks to later generations. These tales and myths give us insight into Celtic Wales and are extremely important because the Celts themselves did not write. Nevertheless, prehistoric Celts remain, to a considerable extent, a mysterious civilization.

Celtic pagan priests, known as the Druids, were held in even higher esteem than the bards. They too memorized vast amounts of information, particularly ritual and dogma. Druids were both male and female and they claimed to be the greatest authorities in Celtic society, each serving as a combination of priest, magician, judge, visionary and diplomat. When they made a decision, they enforced it with threats of spells and curses that swayed even kings and warriors to follow their command.

The legacy of Druidical religion is highly romanticized. Celts believed in a great variety of deities, magical spells, curses and spiritual forces that could be either good or evil. Druids were supposed to be able to commune with the dead in order to foretell the future. Celtic gods could appear in various forms, often disguised as animals. One terrible aspect of this religion was human sacrifice, supposedly prompted by the belief that certain gods could be propitiated only by ritual murder, either by drowning, hanging, burning or stabbing. Druids were alleged to have officiated at sacrificial altars in the midst of stone circles. The most famous of these sites is Stonehenge in England. Some sources hint at a headhunting cult that warriors carried on similar to that of some natives in New Guinea in recent history. Of course, some of the most frightening accounts of Celtic religion can be attributed to the gratuitous exaggerations of the Christian monks who transcribed stories from the pagan Celts.

The Celtic Legacy in Later Centuries

Thanks to busy medieval scribes who toiled in the monasteries, much of Celtic culture was preserved for the attention of later generations. The most famous of them was Geoffrey of Monmouth, who wrote a history of the kings of Britain in the 12th century that included some legends, fantasy and classical references to Wales and the Welsh.

What the monks preserved about Celtic culture was nevertheless allowed to gather dust in libraries, museums and miscellaneous collections for centuries. Early Welsh culture was largely neglected in Wales itself until the late 17th and the early 18th century. At that time antiquarians, people who studied ancient relics as a hobby, appeared and became what are called "Celtophiles," or those who appreciate the Celts. They sought to revive the tradition of the bards but in doing so, they added some of their own tall tales to the Celtic past. The worst was the untrue assertion that the English had sought to end the tradition of the bards by murdering them.

"Celtophobes," or those who disparaged the Celtic past, also appeared. They castigated the early Welsh culture as rife with superstition and sedition and refused to believe the authenticity of many episodes of Celtic history proclaimed by the Celtophiles.

A Celtic revival occurred in the late 18th century as tides of romanticism swept Europe. Romantics everywhere treasured myths, legends and what they called suppressed nationalities. It is no wonder that many romantics were fascinated by Celtic culture. By the 19th century, Celtic studies were well established in British university life. Courses, journals and academic posts came to be based upon Celtic literature, language and archaeology. Celtic studies continued to find a special niche in British intellectual life in the 20th century. The Centre for Advanced Welsh and Celtic Studies at Aberystwyth was established in 1985.

In recent decades a much more intense second Celtic revival has occurred outside the realms of academic life. It is a virtual explosion of enthusiasm for everything Celtic: music, dance, art, design, folklore, poetry and language. It also involves a strong romantic attachment to the Celtic heritage, a fascination with mysticism, and an appreciation of animist spirituality. This revival is linked to many contemporary causes, including the nationalist movement in Wales, the ecological movement and New Age neo-paganism. Moreover, some adherents abroad have become the "Celts of Cyberspace."

A plausible explanation of this powerful Celtic revival is that it serves as an outlet for people who suffer the strains and stresses of modern civilization. The Celtic past is esteemed by them as the beneficial world before civilization. Many of the devotees of the Celtic revival try to follow what they call "the old Druid way," going so far as to participate in elaborate rituals wearing costumes and robes. Many observe Celtic seasonal festivals and practice Wiccan, or white magic.

There is even a Superbowl or World Series of Celtic culture, the Welsh national Eisteddfod, where poets and performers celebrate the ancient language. Included in the pageantry is a leader called the Archdruid and a governing council called the Assembly of bards and maidens who dance with flowers and mistletoe.

Devotees of the Celtic revival, Welsh or from other parts of the world, will enjoy the Celtica Centre at Machynlleth in Powys. It was founded in 1992 in an old noble residence. Everything in it is presented in both Welsh and English. It praises the Celtic inheritance as "a magical blend of myth and music, landscape and language." The Celts are depicted as "husbands of the earth" who live in "openness of spiritual time." Visitors even have the opportunity to travel through a magical forest to a place called the "Otherworld."

The movement has aroused skeptics, who are perhaps neo-Celtophobes. Some grumble about Welsh Celtic celebrations as the "madness going on in Druid-land." They see the Celtic revival as counter to the dominant interests and methods of the cultural and intellectual establishment of the United Kingdom. Yet even the most skeptical of visitors to Wales must acknowledge that something of a Celtic mist still lingers in Wales. The Welsh certainly still cherish music, poetry and provocative conversation, which were all noted characteristics of the ancient Celts. Learned persons and artists are honored in Welsh society more than in most other parts of the Western world, which is another extension of the Celtic past.

Roman Wales — 73 A.D. to *circa* 450 A.D.

The undulating green plains of southern England lured a succession of conquering invaders from the sea up until early modern times. The Romans came in orderly amphibious assaults and conquered the Celts in the 1st century of the Christian era. After approximately four hundred years of occupation and colonization, the Romans were swamped by floods of Anglo-Saxons that poured in from 450 to 600 A.D. and they, in turn, were overcome by the Normans in 1066. All of these invaders eventually sent their forces to the less inviting hill country to the west where the Celtic Welsh were forced to meet them in battle. The Romans and Normans were successful against the Welsh, but the Anglo-Saxons were held off for centuries. The Roman occupation of Wales was superficial and the Norman conquest was piecemeal and confined to southern Wales. The Anglo-Saxons did not settle in Wales in numbers until the Industrial Revolution of modern times. Wales has a history of the preservation of its culture through resistance to invaders. This is why the Welsh have been able to see themselves as the last of the true Britons, still speaking the ancient language of the Celts.

Wales was on the outer periphery of the Roman establishment in Britain and Roman Britain itself was a remote frontier of that great Mediterranean-centered

21

ancient civilization. On the continent romanization was deeper and more thorough than in Britain. There Celtic cultures disappeared completely in many old Celtic lands. In Britain and Ireland, Celtic culture survived because only a few Romans came to occupy Britain while Ireland was judged too remote and unimportant for conquest. Moreover, romanization was tied to urbanization, and the Celts of Britain and Wales remained overwhelmingly rural. Rome's rich civilization, advanced in law, technology, literacy and culture, had only a minimal impact in what the Romans considered a remote, cold and distant island. The end result was that after 400 years of occupation, nearly everything that Rome had sought to install in Britain was demolished by masses of barbarians.

A thin layer of Roman officials, traders and administrators did come to work in Britain. They elevated Latin to become the most important language for those relatively few Celts who took up Roman ways in order to get ahead and improve their standard of living. Romans urged them to live in the relatively few towns they established in Britain, which were all laid out in precise grids. Other Celts rose up against the imposition of Roman rule from time to time, necessitating a permanent Roman military occupation to the north and west.

Wales was one of Rome's military zones, containing three garrison towns, each with a compliment of 6,000 heavily armed foot soldiers who could move around quickly thanks to the Roman skill and persistence in building a network of hundreds of miles of military roads. The Romans also constructed over two-dozen small forts in Wales. Contemporary Welsh place names with *caer* in them indicates an origin as a Roman fortification. Some served as coastal defenses against barbarian attacks from across the Irish Sea.

Relatively little is known about the swift and thorough Roman conquest of Wales, which took place from 73 to 76 A.D. The most celebrated incident was the amphibious campaign against the island of Anglesey, which became a refuge and headquarters for the Druids of Wales. The Druid religion was suppressed by the Romans and their sacred groves on that island were leveled. By the time the Romans finished, all of modern Wales was under their control, marking the first time that all of Wales had ever been united under one political authority.

The occupation of Wales does not seem to have been difficult for the Romans, nor was it difficult for the Celts who, for the most part, pursued their traditional way of life without being disturbed by the military occupation. This was particularly true in the west and north. Wales was economically beneficial for the Romans, who mined and exported some copper, lead, iron and gold from the region.

The Roman legacy for Wales was slight, considering that the Romans controlled Wales for hundreds of years. Agrarian practices certainly did improve, allowing higher yields per acre on the best Welsh farmland. Also, a substantial number of Latin words were mixed into the Welsh language over time.

Christianity was one of the many new religions the Romans brought to Wales, and it survived into the Dark Ages, but just how many Celtic Christians there were remains a subject of considerable conjecture. There were probably not many of them. The strongest aspect of

Rome's legacy was in the field of their greatest expertise and accomplishment: engineering. Some of the roads, forts and water systems they built in Wales stayed in service until the 19th century.

The Isle of Angelsey, Llanddwyn Island.
COURTESY OF THE WALES TOURIST BOARD.

Wales in the Dark Ages
and After — 450 to 1066

The Dark Ages saw the slow crumbling of the Roman Empire and the conquests of the Germanic barbarians throughout Western Civilization from France to North Africa. Once the barbarians settled and became converts to Christianity, the official religion of the Roman Empire in its final centuries, they sought to carry on with a crude imitation of Roman ways in their various kingdoms. From this amalgamation of Roman, Christian and barbarian elements, medieval civilization emerged. Medieval is an adjective for the Middle Ages, a time span between the fall of Rome and the rebirth of elements of classic ancient civilization the era of the Renaissance and Reformation. The Middle Ages span roughly the period from 500 A.D. to 1500 A.D., a thousand years. The Dark Ages themselves comprise the early part of the Middle Ages, roughly from around 450 to 800 A.D. For the island of Britain it is something of a blank page in history. The invaders were illiterate and therefore nothing was written down about these times until centuries later, long after myths and legends about the time had grown.

In the rough, tumultuous centuries, when the elements of medieval civilization were in gestation, the part of Britain that became England suffered the most thorough barbarian conquest. The Anglo-Saxons simply obliterated Rome's legacy on the open lands and forests of the rolling English plains. They were Germanic pagans who thoroughly destroyed England's early Christian establishment. They were noted as tall, blonde, ferocious warriors who lived in tightly organized tribes. England's Celtic population was conquered, slaughtered, or driven out into to the hill country to the north and west. Those Celtic exiles who were romanized found that it was impossible to maintain the civilization they had adopted in rugged, agrarian areas. Romanization could only survive in urban settings.

This troubled, tumultuous era was devoid of writing and significant archaeological remains. Therefore everything we know about this period remains tangled in myths, misrepresentations and thin historical theories. Some Welsh nationalists have idealized the Dark Ages as a time of glorious independence, when the Welsh nationality was strengthened. But, regardless of distortions and exaggerations based upon meager historical evidence, it is undeniable that the Dark Ages had a profound impact on Welsh history. The superficial influence of Rome on what was really a marginal part of their empire faded rapidly once direct Roman rule ended in the first decades of the 5th century.

For the first time, Celtic Wales became a geographic entity as the barbarians pushed to the north and west and isolated the Celts of Wales from other Celtic peoples. Before the Anglo-Saxons, Celtic tribes and alliances had extended far beyond the borders of contemporary Wales. The Anglo-Saxons pushed the Celts back, confined them, and kept them under attack. Wales became a Celtic refuge. The border was established along the rough, wet, hilly and mountainous region west of the Severn River, the very border between England and Wales for all subsequent centuries. The Anglo-Saxons took only the warmer, more fertile and drier lands to the east. Eventually they gave their name to this area as Angeland, which later became England.

The Anglo-Saxons were not the only source of danger. Fierce Picts, a Celtic people, raided in the north and Celtic Irish seafarers struck at coastal Wales. Meanwhile, Celtic tribal chiefs began to evolve as the precursors of Welsh princes and petty kings. Eventually close to twenty such rulers emerged. Yet the subjects of all of these rulers were evolving into a distinct people, simultaneously called the Cymry, which the English called the Welsh, a corruption from their word for stranger, *Wealas*.

One Anglo-Saxon king, Offa, ruler of a kingdom called Mercia, defined the border between Wales and England. He wished to protect Anglo-Saxon farming settlements from Welsh raiders. In the late 8th century he constructed a rampart along the Welsh frontier known as Offa's Dike. It runs roughly from the estuary of the Severn River, which empties into the Bristol Channel, up to the River Dee in the north, a total of 149 miles. It was the most impressive human-made boundary in Europe, a rampart averaging 6 feet high and 60 feet wide. The dike has served as a boundary between Wales and England for 1000 years and much of it remains to this day as an impressive ancient monument.

When the Celtic peoples were isolated from each other by the Anglo-Saxons, their languages evolved and changed and became separate, although still linked in a Celtic language family. Nevertheless, the Welsh of Wales, the Cornish of Cornwall, the Gaelic of Scotland, the Breton of Brittany and the Irish of Ireland all differentiated in pronunciation, vocabulary and grammar. Welsh, called Cymraeg, was fused with many Latin expressions drawn from the early Christian Church.

Another profound change for Wales during the Dark Ages was the firm rooting of Christianity. Some romanized Welsh had been Christians, but it is believed that they were very few in number and that their new religion was not very widespread and therefore only had a weak presence at the beginning of the Dark Ages. It took the activities of missionaries in the 6th century to bring about widespread conversions. They were Celtic missionaries from recently converted Ireland and Brittany who wandered about Wales, preaching and converting. In these troubled times, Christianity came to provide some cultural coherence throughout Wales.

Many of the early practitioners of Celtic Christianity were ascetic, meaning that they lived lives of deliberate deprivation. Coastal areas and islands became religious sites for them. Incidentally, the only monuments surviving this period of early Welsh Christianity today are Celtic stone crosses.

The patron saint of Wales, the equivalent of St. Patrick in Ireland, St. George in England and St. Andrew in Scotland, appeared at this time. He was St. David, who is shrouded in myth and legend. All sorts of miracles and wondrous deeds are attributed to him, including a direct confrontation with the devil himself. He supposedly went on pilgrimages to England and even to distant Jerusalem. He lived in the 6th century and may have died in 589 A.D. He did found churches in many parts of Wales, including what became the site of St. David's Cathedral. Pilgrimages to the site became popular in later centuries and his saint's day, St. David's Day, March 1, became an important Welsh holiday that is still celebrated.

Both the English and the Welsh claim another mythical figure from the Dark Ages, the legendary King Arthur. The stories and legends surrounding him were written much later than the time he lived, which was in the late 5th or early 6th centuries. Therefore he has gone down in popular history as a Christian king of the Middle Ages who lived when knighthood was in full flower rather than centuries before, when Christians fought invading barbarians. In all probability, he was a romanized Celtic Briton who adopted and upheld Roman Christian civilization against the pagan Anglo-Saxons. This would certainly give the romanized Welsh a claim to regard him as their champion and for Welsh people to do the same in later centuries.

The Vikings, another fierce pagan people, descended upon Britain from Scandinavia in the 9th century. By this time, both the Welsh and the English, as the Anglo-Saxons were now known, had become Christians. In fact, Welsh leaders formed some temporary alliances with English kingdoms to resist the new onslaught on their lands. The Vikings did not attack Wales as heavily as England and Ireland because they regarded the area as poorer for plundering or settling. Even so, the names Anglesey and Swansea are of Scandinavian origin. When

Legendary King Arthur during his Coronation as a Medieval King.

the bordering English kingdom of Mercia temporarily fell to the Danes, the Welsh were able to enjoy a long period of isolation from England, which fostered the separate development of their institutions, language, and law.

Up until the Viking raids, the Welsh were divided into a large number of small kingdoms called Gwledydd, stretched across Wales as a quilt of unstable entities. The political history of this time is indeed a period of much confusion. Wales was fragmented throughout the Dark Ages, and whatever amalgamations were achieved by this or that ruler would be undone in the next generation.

The Viking threat certainly brought many Welsh kingdoms together, and some acknowledged Anglo-Saxon rulers as their overlords for the sake of protection. Even so, one of the recurring themes in Welsh history in this very early period was the desire to form an alliance of Celtic peoples to oppose Anglo-Saxon overlordship. This aspiration seems to have been most strongly held in the area of Gwynedd in the northwest of Wales, the area long since acknowledged as the heartland of the Welsh national identity.

Just before the Norman conquest of England, one Welsh prince was noted for his brutality. Grufudd Ap Llywellyn (1039–1065) went on rampages against his neighbors and even drove out his English neighbors beyond Offa's Dike. For a brief, transitory time he controlled all of Wales. He married a noble lady from the Anglo-Saxon kingdom of Mercia and allied with Mercia against the Kingdom of the West Saxons.

It took a campaign by the Saxon prince Harold Godwinson, the future king of England, famous for falling in battle before William the Conqueror at Hastings in 1066, to drive Llywellyn to the remote mountain fastness of northwest Wales. There he was assassinated by a Welshman seeking revenge for his depredations against his family. Harold nevertheless married Llywellyn's widow, Ealdgyth, a woman who began as Queen of Wales and who became Queen of England. Wales once again had a temporary, transitory unity under one ruler, but this would all suddenly change just over a year later when the Normans stormed ashore on the southern coast of England.

Most ordinary Welsh people were undoubtedly unaffected by the triumphs, alliances and failures of the petty kingdoms. Their blood relations were most important to them. Relatives were connected in extended families and larger tribal groups and pedigrees of descent were cherished. For most people, life in the Dark Ages was hard and short, and filled with unending, repetitious toil on the land and mortal dangers from violence and disease. Most people spent most of their time living close to a subsistence level, fearful of the times when bad harvests from their small farms might push them into starvation. In the lowlands of Wales some Medieval manors were established, places where a local leader would carry on farming with the help of men securely bonded to the land and protected by him. In the uplands of Wales free communities carried on a pastoral economy, tending flocks and herds of animals.

Christianity provided consolations for the hard-pressed ordinary people of Wales. The church offered hope for a better life after death, a day of rest each week, some holy days, which became holidays, and a glimpse of majesty and the miraculous in the local church every Sunday. The church also promoted peace and obedience in those troubled times.

Wales from the Norman Conquest to the Edwardian Conquest — 1068 to 1277

One of the most famous dates in English history is 1066, the year that the Norman King, William the Conqueror, or, as he was known to his detractors, William the Bastard, defeated the Anglo-Saxons and began a rapid conquest of their country. While swiftness and brutality were the hallmarks of the Norman conquest of England, their enterprise in Wales was much more of a gradual assertion of power. Yet for both England and Wales, the impact of the Normans was highly significant and permanent. They imposed the feudal system on England and on large portions of Wales. This meant a new organization of law, administration, farming and religion, which had the effect of bringing most of Britain into line with medieval organization on the continent of Europe.

Just who were the Normans? They were formidable predators who came from Normandy, a seacoast province of France. Yet they were non-French in origin. They were originally called Northmen because they came from Scandinavia as seething, restless conquerors. In France they learned new methods of fighting and ruling in just over one hundred years before they invaded England. Never very numerous, they imposed themselves as a French-speaking, mounted, ruling elite who protected themselves by networks of relatively simple castles. Over

A Medieval depiction of Norman Soldiers aboard a ship.

the centuries, they gradually assimilated with the English and Welsh. The English language today is clear evidence of this blending: the Germanic vocabulary from the Anglo-Saxons has been amalgamated with the Latin French vocabulary from the Normans. Just as the languages blended, the Norman French stock was absorbed into the much more numerous Anglo-Saxon population to produce a nationality forever known as "the English."

England went down before them in just a few years, but there was no Norman conquest of Wales as such. Instead there were isolated invasions by various Norman lords who seized and occupied lands in Wales. Therefore, the Norman invasion of Wales was much more of a piecemeal operation and it was only pursued in southern and eastern parts of Wales.

William the Conqueror himself campaigned in Wales in 1068, but decided that he would rather have a barrier between his English lands and the fierce Welsh. He also wanted to reward his victorious Norman commanders. Therefore he granted Welsh lands as earldoms for his close kinsmen and followers. They became known as "marcher lordships," and their holdings as the Marches of Wales. A march was a difficult border region where local rulers were granted unusual autonomy by the monarch, meaning that they enjoyed more rights and freedom to govern the area than lords would have in England. At worst, the marcher lords became robber barons who held sway over their regions by force and fear. The marches were places where the king's writ, or the king's lawful orders, did not run. The area therefore had a reputation for lawlessness, but in actuality, the "Law of the March" came to be applied by the Norman lords. This was actually local Welsh law as interpreted by the Normans and often applied with a ruthless cruelty. Moreover, they could build castles and wage war, but the king of England did not have to help them when they were in difficulty.

Half a century after the Normans landed in England, one quarter of Wales was held by Norman barons in the name of the kings of England. Their castles dotted the landscape of eastern and southern Wales. The most famous of these marcher lordships were in the border counties of Hereford, Shrewsbury and Chester. The Earl of Shrewsbury, whose family name was Montgomery, made a spectacular advance in Wales and reached the sea, where he established the castle at Pembroke. Yet he became rebellious and eventually the king seized his castle and gave it to Gilbert de Clare, the first Earl of Pembroke.

Marcher lordships in Wales were dynamic and expanding entities containing restless and ambitious young Norman warriors. The next Earl of Pembroke, known to history as "Strongbow," led an expedition of restless, land-hungry Normans from Wales to intervene in a dynastic dispute in Ireland in the 12th century. This was, in fact, the very beginning of the Norman English conquest of Ireland.

There remained a sharp contrast between Norman England and Norman Wales. The Norman kingdom in England was noted for its centralized nature, and for what was, for the Middle Ages, an efficient system of administration and law. By contrast, Norman Wales dispersed authority in a mosaic of lordships.

Despite all of their energy and ability, the Normans did not subdue Wales. Instead, they partitioned it. The marcher area was called "Marchia Walliae," the March of Wales, and the independent part of Wales gained the name *Wallia pura* or native Wales, or pure Wales. This tangible sphere of native influence covered more than half of the surface of Wales and was governed by a number of independent Welsh rulers. Nevertheless, they did have to express homage and fealty to the distant English crown. From the time of William the Conqueror, both Welsh princes and Norman marcher lords had to send their tribute, or small amounts of money, similar to paying dues, to the Norman kings of England. Outside of this tribute, which was actually a formality, the Welsh in *Wallia pura* carried on their own culture and way of life. Therefore, in the Middle Ages, a frontier existed between Norman Welshness and Welsh Welshness, and the effects of this division have lasted until the present day.

Wallia pura was a region where the Norman barons ordinarily did not intrude. It remained the most Welsh part of the country, with its heartland in Gwynedd in the north. This region was the bastion of Welsh culture in the Middle Ages, and it has remained so, becoming the bastion of Welsh nationalism in the modern age.

One basic reason for this division of Norman Wales and Welsh Wales was economic. The Normans needed low-lying land with good soil and a fairly moderate climate to establish their traditional large scale farming on feudal estates. Only eastern and southern Wales afforded them such opportunities. They therefore left the wetter and rougher lands to the north and west to the Welsh rulers.

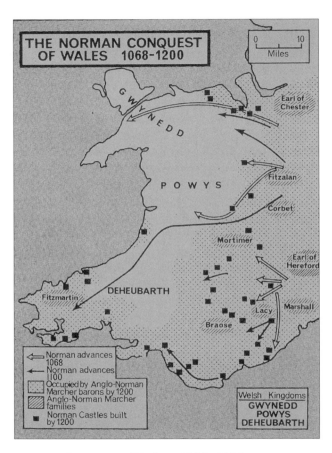

Norman Conquest of Wales, 1068–1208.

The establishment of Norman manors required that thousands of Welsh farmers become Norman serfs; people bound to the land and required to render goods and services to their lords. This was the nature of feudalism throughout Europe. In return for their bondage, the serfs were protected in their right to sharecropping of certain lands and to pass this arrangement on to their heirs. Many Welsh resisted the push into serfdom and fled to the hills where they carried on a more primitive and less productive form of agriculture on less valuable lands. When the manors were established many prominent and ancient local Welsh families were humiliated and thrust from their holdings and replaced by Norman lords.

Great manors were not the only economic changes brought by the Normans. Small, fortified towns also appeared in the areas where the Normans established their feudal operations. Norman merchants, craftsmen and ex-soldiers settled in these towns and began to carry on modest trading with other locations. In particular, the exportation of cattle to England became important. Most towns came to have a market, a huddle of shops and houses and a church. Nearby a Norman castle was likely to stand, made of earth and timber, guarded by ditches, and known as a "motte and bailey" castle. Eventually, the Normans brought in administrators, churchmen and monks to Wales. In Pembroke a number of Flemish colonists arrived and replaced the local Welsh, beginning Pembroke's reputation as "Little England Beyond Wales." Before the Normans, Wales had no medieval towns.

The Normans came to England blessed by the pope and under the impression that they were great churchmen who could reform the Christian church throughout Britain and bring it into line with the order and discipline of the ever growing and strengthening medieval Roman Catholic Church on the Continent. The church in Wales was brought into line by eliminating old Celtic Christian practices, such as allowing some clergy to marry and changing various details, such as holidays on the church calendar. Bishops in Wales were put under the authority of the Archbishop of Canterbury and all bishops appointed in the future were to be individuals favoring Norman rule.

A large number of monastic houses were founded: Benedictine, Augustinian and Cistercian. The Cistercian order was particularly well-suited to Wales because they preferred remote mountain areas and sheep farming. Monasteries were built in both Marcher Wales and *Wallia pura.* Every Welsh prince of importance in *Wallia pura* helped found a Cistercian monastic abbey in his territory.

The establishment of monasteries throughout Wales was very beneficial for Welsh culture. The monks were eager to study, copy and preserve ancient Welsh literature. One of the most famous Welsh churchmen was Gerald of Wales, known in Latin as Geraldus Cambrensis, who lived from 1146 to 1223. His identity is ambiguous because of his mixed Norman and Welsh lineage; he felt himself a Norman among the Welsh and a Welshman among the Normans (much as an Anglo-Irishman would be considered an Englishman among the Irish and an Irishman among the English.) His education took him out of Wales to England and France, but he returned to hold various church livings. He traveled throughout Wales and wrote extensively about what he saw, becoming one of Wales' greatest writers in Latin, a man who was called the first famous non-Welsh speaking Welshmen.

Another famous churchman from Wales, already mentioned, was Geoffrey of Monmouth, who lived a century and a half earlier. He was a scholar who spent most of his life in England, at Oxford. But he did write a history of the ancient Britons and passed on myths that many Welsh would treasure. According to him, an ancient Trojan king was the ancestor of the Welsh and the first ruler to unify Britain. From this came the idea that a Welsh leader had a moral right to the throne of England. This myth was actually celebrated and used as a justification in the 16th century by the Welsh House of Tudor as it lay claim to the throne of England.

All during the time that the Normans held sway in part of Wales, the ordinary people they ruled sought to carry on Welsh culture and family traditions. Nevertheless, intermarriage of Welsh women with Norman men often took place, blending the two cultures. At the same time, Normans adopted Welsh lifestyles, just as they would adopt Irish lifestyles in Ireland. What went on over the centuries was really a two-way cultural diffusion as the Welsh and Normans adopted many aspects of their respective ways of life.

This piecemeal physical and cultural invasion of Wales by the Normans was not all peaceful. There was Welsh resistance. Guerrilla fighting against the Norman lords went on regularly, and sometimes, Norman kings of England would send expeditions to Wales to help marcher lords. The Welsh princedoms to the north and west offered more organized resistance. In the 10th century a Welsh prince named Owain Ap Gruffudd (1137–1170) expanded his control over the Welsh heartland and actually recovered some areas from the marcher lords.

One of the most intelligent and effective of all English medieval kings, Henry II, who ruled from 1154 to 1189, made a military incursion into Wales. Yet he really preferred to win over the Welsh princes by giving them offices of importance in the feudal system. Wherever he went, he sought to impress the Welsh with royal pomp and ceremony. This exercise of the English monarchy has not ceased to the present day.

One confrontation between Henry II and an old native Welshman was recorded in a medieval chronicle. This story is treasured by Welsh nationalists to the present day. It is said that Henry II was told by the native Welshman that "the Welsh people will never be destroyed except by the anger of God alone for, on the Day of Judgment, no people or nation other than that of Wales will answer before the Supreme Judge for this little corner of the world." Later King Henry II wrote in a letter to the Byzantine Emperor that "the Welsh are a people who cannot be tamed."

Two Welshmen, both named Llewelyn of Gwynedd, one Llewelyn the Great and the other Llewelyn the Last, were also notable for their resistance. Llewelyn the Great, or Llewelyn ap Iowerth, was Prince of Gwynedd from 1194 to 1240. He made common cause with the new English dynasty, the Plantagenets, and married an illegitimate daughter of an English king. He gained control over most of the lesser Welsh princes and sought to build up a more centralized Welsh government modeled in part on England's monarchy. For a time he was able to unite the Welsh

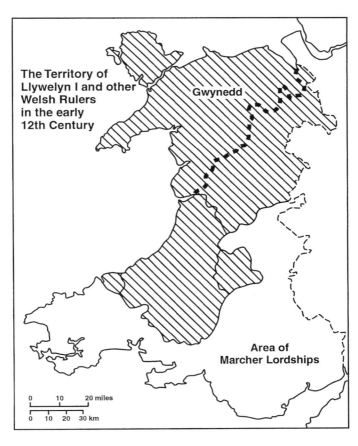

The Territory of
Llywelyn I and other
Welsh Rulers
in the early
12th Century

Gwynedd

Area of
Marcher Lordships

0   10   20 miles

0   10   20   30 km

Map of Welsh rulers.

in *Wallia pura* and present the region as a principality with an effective Prince of Wales. Nevertheless he had to pay tribute and offer homage to the distant English king.

When the English barons rose against the oppressions of King John, Llewelyn joined them and held Shrewsbury at the time that the king was forced to sign that most famous document of the Middle Ages, Magna Carta, in 1215. He championed one of its clauses that specifically allowed Welsh law in *Wallia pura*, Marcher Law in the Marches and English law just in England, thus indicating the strong attachment of the Welsh to their own law and culture.

Llewelyn the Last unfortunately confronted a much more powerful English king who was bent on crushing Wales once and for all. The forces of Edward I of England captured and killed this last Welsh Prince of Wales in 1282.

The Edwardian Conquest
of Wales — 1277 to 1290

Edward I, one of the most able and strongest English kings, had a massive effect on the history of Wales, spiritually and physically. Edward I (1272–1307) was controversial in his lifetime and thereafter, like so many other striking rulers in history. Many see him as the enlightened ruler who modernized the common law through a whirlwind of legal activity. The king was certainly at the center of a huge amount of litigation, legislation and judgment. He also took the development of Parliament many steps forward by broadening its representation.

The Welsh and Scots of his time did not see him in this light. For them he was a determined and ruthless military leader, bent on overwhelming conquest. Although he failed to subdue Scotland, he succeeded dramatically in Wales.

Conquerors almost always manage to blame the conquered for initiating their aggression. In the case of Edward I's great campaign against Wales in 1277, the blame was put upon Llywelyn II, or Llywelyn ap Gruffudd, also known as Llywelyn the Last. Edward I's father, Henry III, had acknowledged him as the Prince of Wales. He had participated in the English civil wars preceding Edward's reign. He was accused of breaching a treaty he signed to give up control of some shires and being slow

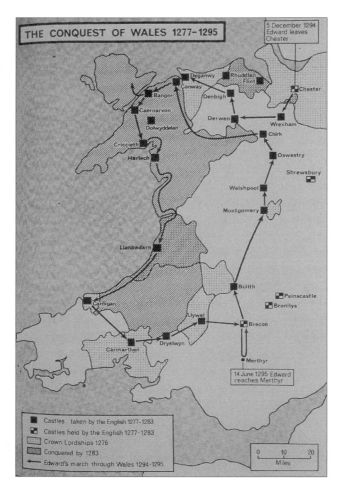

The following labels appear on the map:

THE CONQUEST OF WALES 1277–1295

5 December 1294
Edward leaves
Chester

Deganwy
Rhuddlan
Flint
Conway
Bangor
Denbigh
Chester
Caernarvon
Derwen
Dolwyddelan
Wrexham
Criccieth
Chirk
Harlech
Oswestry
Shrewsbury
Welshpool
Montgomery
Llanbadarn
Builth
Painscastle
Bronllys
Cardigan
Llywel
Brecon
Drysllwyn
Carmarthen
Merthyr

14 June 1295 Edward
reaches Merthyr

Castles taken by the English 1277-1283
Castles held by the English 1277-1283
Crown Lordships 1276
Conquered by 1283
Edward's march through Wales 1294-1295

0   10   20
Miles

The Edwardian Conquest of Wales, 1277–1295.

to offer homage and obedience to the new English king. Llywelyn also sought marriage in an English family aligned against Edward.

As in so many confrontations, the Welsh and English viewed Llywelyn II differently. While a Welsh monk could write that he was a "pure character" who was "radiant in lawful power," an English scribe called him "a prince of errors, a traitor, thief, firebrand, evil genius" and a "source of every ill."

The subsequent English invasion was out of all proportion to the cause. Edward marched all through Wales with a large, complex army. It included mercenaries hired by loans taken in Italian banks; the English feudal host, consisting of those obligated to do homage by serving him in war; and a corps of specialized archers and cross-bowmen utilizing the latest military techniques. His large army was supported by a vast logistical force of masons, miners, woodmen and reapers.

The English invasion marched overland and also came by sea, supported throughout the campaign by an Anglo-French fleet. Wherever they marched and wherever they occupied the countryside, they disrupted Welsh agriculture by requisitioning food supplies, often by reaping crops in the fields themselves.

Llywelyn II became Llywelyn the Last when he fell in battle in 1282, supposedly after his position was betrayed to the English by another Welshman. His head was cut off and sent to the king, who paraded it through the streets of London and had it stuck up in public view on the Tower of London, which was not an uncommon way of dealing with those proscribed as traitors. For Wales it was a dramatic beginning of a new era.

Welsh resistance was crushed time and again. Wherever a strong point was perceived, the English king built a castle and linked it with military roads. These giant structures, today the pride of travel pamphlets on Wales, were the key bastions for the military domination and English civilian governance of what had been *Wallia pura*, or independent Wales. Edward built eight major new castles in Wales and repaired several old ones extensively. They were at key locations, linked by military roads and capable of being supplied and reinforced by sea.

These beautiful, powerful castles are some of the most remarkable Medieval monuments in all of Europe. One castle alone, Caerphilly, covered twenty-five acres. They remain famous far beyond Wales: Harlech, Conway Caernarvon, Criccieth, and many others. To quote a Welsh observer, they have remained "the magnificent badges of our subjection."

Sometimes the towns around them were swiftly walled and linked to the edifice. Conway is an excellent example of this kind of construction. Major new towns, called boroughs, were built by Edward, including Aberystwyth, Rhuddlan, Caernafron, Harlech, Criccieth and Beaumaris.

What is so surprising about this building program is the speed with which it was carried out. In an age when it might take centuries to build a cathedral, Edward's legions of workers constructed or repaired an iron ring of fourteen castles from Aberystwyth to Flint in a few years. The mountain mass of northwest Wales became

Top: *A view of contemporary Conway from the air today.*
Bottom: *A view of Conway Castle today with a Victorian railway bridge.*

ringed with English strong points. Huge importations of stone, lead, iron, steel, rope and timber came from all over Edward's realm. Immense English resources were expended on this program, whose modern equivalent might be the construction of a force of nuclear submarines and intercontinental missiles.

It took more than one operation to master the area. Another campaign from 1282 to 1283 included an amphibious assault to capture the large Welsh island of Anglesey. Meanwhile, English forces marched in a three-pronged attack: they came along the northern shore, the west coast and through the very center of Wales. Welshmen who continued to resist were eventually hunted down in the hills.

All of this activity in Wales drained the English treasury and thereby had an influence on the development of English constitutional history. Edward was required to call many Parliaments and grant concessions to their English lords and representatives in order to get them to grant the extra funds needed for his conquests. Furthermore, he pressed the clergy to give him gifts and borrowed heavily.

The effect on Scotland could have been as profound. Why was Edward I able to conquer Wales so effectively and then fail to conquer Scotland? This is one of the enduring questions about the reign of this great English monarch. Surely, both Wales and Scotland were much weaker, much poorer and much more lightly populated than the prosperous and well-governed kingdom of England. Some have cited the collaboration of marcher lords and some petty Welsh leaders with the invading English forces. Yet this situation also prevailed in Scotland where there were also keen divisions among native rulers. Certainly one important difference between Wales and Scotland was the compact nature of Welsh geography. By contrast to *Wallia pura*, Scotland was a large area with a consequently larger population, even if it was thinly distributed. Another important factor was the Scottish alliance with France that prevailed at the time.

The very success of the English in mastering Wales has also been cited as a cause for the failure to vanquish Scotland. Edward's expenditure on subduing and occupying Wales was lavish, thereby subtracting from the resources that could be marshaled for the campaigns in Scotland.

The Welsh suffered the fate of many defeated peoples— a dictated peace which was imposed by the Statute of Rhuddlan of 1284. This notable document established principles for governing Wales. All the Welsh were declared to be subjects of the English crown and the large part of Wales under royal control was divided into shires, the unit of county division that had long prevailed in England. In these shires the apparatus of English governance was introduced, consisting of English sheriffs, English courts and English criminal law. Civil law, or law between subject and subject over such things as land and other property, was allowed to remain based on old Welsh law and it continued in use until the 16th century. New royal officials, justices with various titles, were appointed. Most of Wales had never had these institutions and officers before.

Many historians have praised the efforts of Edward I to extend the royal law of England to Wales. In some ways it was similar to how the British Empire of recent centuries imposed its legal system over the varied local laws of indigenous peoples with utter confidence in its superiority. As in Wales, the colonized peoples had no choice in the matter. Yet when independence finally came in the 20th century, most ex-colonial areas, such as India, retained both English law and the English language on the basis of familiarity and utility.

Even in England royal law was regarded as superior to local, manorial law in providing justice for the lesser subjects of the crown. Manorial law was controlled by the particular local lord of the manor who might have prejudiced interests in the proceedings. The innovations of English law, such as the jury system, the right of *habeas corpus*, or the right to a speedy trial, and due process are landmarks in the evolution of justice. After the conquest, the part of Wales controlled by the crown enjoyed what arguably was the most advanced and efficient system of justice in Europe. Whatever else may be said of Edward I, his skill in fostering the law in his realm is undeniable. In Wales as in England, his settlement was thorough and coherent.

Those parts of Wales under the control of marcher lords were not divided into shires. Edward did not annex the March of Wales. In fact, he created new, independent marcher lordships to reward the most important barons that helped him conquer Wales. They themselves were entrusted with the task of pacifying and settling their portions of the Welsh countryside. Meanwhile the old marcher lords took back lands that had slipped from their grasp and even encroached beyond their old boundaries. The perpetuation of the old division of Wales between the marches and the north continued. So did the marchers' contempt for the Welsh in the northern hills and mountains.

There were a few ineffective Welsh rebellions after the Edwardian conquest, and these were dealt with harshly. Rebellious communities were heavily fined and punitive ordinances were proclaimed in 1295. These harsh, discriminatory ordinances reached their culmination after the great rebellion of Owen Glendower in the early 15th century.

Despite whatever benefits may have come from the application of English law, it is clear that Edward's conquest marked the beginning colonial treatment for the Welsh in what had been *Wallia pura.* The English assumed that their settlers were superior and efforts were made to keep them separated from the Welsh. This was most evident in the establishment of new towns, called boroughs, which were peopled with privileged English immigrants. For a time Welshmen were prohibited from inhabiting the towns and from trading or carrying arms within the walls. There were also restrictions on marriages between the two groups. In effect, English law, English order and English customs were imposed unilaterally and with no regard for the Welshness of the inhabitants.

Direct annexation of Wales would not take place until 1536, under the Tudors, and for the time being Wales remained a separate entity, divided into a principality consisting of crown-controlled lands in the north and central area and a collection of smaller marcher lordships in the south. The principality of Wales would never again be independent. The dynasty of Llywelyn and the families of other Welsh leaders were treated harshly.

Daughters were sent off to nunneries and some sons were imprisoned.

To crown his success, Edward I designated his son and heir as the Prince of Wales. Ever since, right up to the present, the next male in line to the English throne has been designated the Prince of Wales, no matter how English or French or German the ancestry of the royal heir might be. What had been the title of the ruler of Wales now became simply an honorific designation for the next in line to the throne of England.

The first Prince of Wales became the unfortunate and ultimately deposed King Edward II of England. He was born in 1284 at Carnarvon Castle, Edward's administrative center in Wales. The queen and the prince had accompanied Edward I during his triumphant progress through newly conquered Wales. Legend surrounds the event: Edward was supposed to have lifted his infant son on his shield before a multitude of Welsh who asked whether the heir spoke English or Welsh. The king replied that he could not yet speak at all. What makes the story a legend is that the royal family at that time spoke French.

Edward's victory was a crushing, complete conquest, eliminating any possibility of any part of Wales operating as an independent political entity. Henceforth, and until very recently, the only place that Welshness could survive was in the hearts and minds of Welsh people signified by the use of the Welsh language. To be sure, there would be a great rebellion under Owen Glendower 120 years after Edward I's conquest, and his castles would for a time be controlled by the Welsh, but this was only a temporary situation. The English conquest was re-imposed once more thereafter.

Owen Glendower and the
Last Rising — 1400 to 1408

Nostalgic lost causes and leaders have always claimed a romantic place in history. For the Welsh, their mystical, heroic and tragic leader was Owen Glendower, to use his anglicized name. This important landholder and descendant of Welsh ruling dynasties lived from around 1359 and probably died around 1416. He led an extensive rebellion from 1400 to 1408. In 1400, Welshmen proclaimed him Prince of Wales instead of acknowledging an English heir to the English throne in a last attempt of the Welsh to overthrow the English yoke upon their nation.

One recurring theme in the Middle Ages was that the outlying areas of the English crown, Wales, Ireland and Scotland, could maneuver and assert themselves when English fortunes fell. Glendower's rising fit this pattern. The rebellion came at a difficult time for the English crown, just after King Richard II had been deposed in 1399 and presumably brutally murdered by an important faction of nobles. His successor, Henry IV, endured the struggles of a divided English nobility and rival claimants to the throne. It was also a time of division for the Papacy, with two Popes each claiming legitimacy and the right to recognize European rulers. Moreover, the kings of England were not only beset by unrest in Wales.

Scotland, Ireland and France were also hostile, as well as some parts of England, such as Northumbria.

The causes of the rising in Wales were economic and social. There was considerable economic dislocation from the Black Plague, a horrendous malady which struck Wales hard from 1349 to 1350 and again in 1361 and 1369. Most of western Europe suffered similarly from this scourge of nature. In some places the population was reduced by a third or by a half. Nobles found that they faced a labor shortage on their manors as considerable amounts of formerly tilled land went idle. They responded by trying to get even more money from their tenants and more work from their bondmen. The result was widespread discontent. Often the great tenants who could not pay their taxes to the crown had their lands confiscated by royal officials. Some marcher lords were rapidly replaced by royal edict, often by the installation of greedier nobles. Meanwhile, some individuals took advantage of rural economic dislocation by buying up underutilized lands cheaply. From all these causes, the net result of the black plague was an abundance of angry, hard pressed and discontented Welsh eager to rebel.

When a small number of his family and friends declared Owen Glendower Prince of Wales in 1400, a bitter guerrilla struggle broke out that had considerable initial success. He evaded three royal expeditions sent against him while he managed to capture many royal castles. Seeking legitimacy, he quickly summoned an assembly of Welsh leaders and called it a Welsh Parliament. No parliamentary tradition had existed in Wales previously as it had in England. It crowned him Prince of Wales in 1404, a much more impressive event than the proclamation of this status in 1400 by his intimates.

Owen Glendower had always claimed to be a descendant of the ancient Welsh king of the eighth century, Cadwaladr. He also put forward rather grandiose plans to extend a victorious Wales far into England and have a Welsh Parliament sit regularly. In addition, he wanted to create two Welsh universities so that native Welsh could be educated in Wales in order to become the civil servants in his new government. He also wanted to free the church in Wales from English influence, which meant dependency upon the Archbishop of Canterbury. He wanted a Welsh bishop to preside over the church in Wales and to replace Englishmen in church offices with fellow Welshmen. Some local bishops had recognized him and did approve of these plans for the church.

The popularly proclaimed ruler of Wales was able to reign as a sovereign prince for a dozen years, undisturbed by an insecure English monarchy. Owen Glendower cast about for allies for the rebellious Welsh, particularly in Scotland and Northumbria. He also sought an alliance with Edward Mortimer, an important marcher lord. Meanwhile he gained recognition from the French king, who was quite willing to welcome the claims of an enemy of his enemy.

Eventually, the power of the English crown was organized and applied. Noble leaders, men, ships and weapons were gathered in the north at Chester and in the south at Bristol and were sent off to subdue the Welsh rebels. Unfortunately for Glendower, he did not have the loyalty of

St. David's Cathedral, one of the smallest cathedrals in Britain.

all of the Welsh. Some native gentry in the south allied with the English crown instead.

The Welsh fought fiercely and remorselessly in defense, destroying church buildings, homes and even farm animals in English occupied areas. They tried to avoid pitched battles, retreated and did not challenge newly arrived English garrisons in royal castles. Prince Hal of England, who would go on to become Henry V, famous as Shakespeare's warrior king, began to defeat his forces. Gradually, a substantial number of castles were wrested back from the Welsh. Beaten and reduced in numbers, Glendower's forces surrendered in 1414, but he himself never surrendered. Nobody is sure of what eventually became of him. He simply disappeared into the mists of the Welsh mountains, which is perhaps one of the best ways for a romantic Medieval hero to depart from the stage of history. His disappearance enabled a host of legends about him to grow.

Glendower remained a popular, mystical hero for Welsh people for centuries and remains so, in a way, right up to the present. He had all of the characteristics expected for a person in such a role: he was hot-blooded, outspoken and blustering and he wanted to be the sole ruler of all of Wales. He was also a highly capable leader for the times, talented in military tactics and skilled in politics. Despite all of his ambition and temporary achievement, the unity he imposed over most of Wales was merely transitory. Yet he provided a glorious memory for all the patriotic Welsh of all subsequent centuries. His revolt was the very last sustained military struggle against the English conquest of Wales.

Wales in the Late
Middle Ages — 1290 to 1485

The aftermath of Owen Glendower's rising was severe for Wales. Royal officers seized lands and imposed fines. Penal laws, passed by the English Parliament in 1402, sought to punish the rebellious Welsh. Henceforth, the Welsh could not carry weapons, live within major towns, conduct trade or even meet in groups. The Welsh were not to have equality before the law, making it difficult for them to sue Englishmen. The Welsh could not hold any major office in church and state, acquire land, or become a burgess, that is, a member of a town's governing corporation. If an Englishman married a Welsh woman, the same restrictions would apply to him. In short, the Welsh were reduced to second-class citizens.

Colonialism was never more oppressive than in the aftermath of Owen Glendower's rising. As the years went on, most of these laws were overlooked, but they remained on the statute books as an embarrassment to the Welsh. Many upcoming substantial Welsh landholders, called the gentry, were the most affronted by this discrimination. They sought redress at law, petitioning to be "made English." Many were exempted from the penal laws by this practice. Meanwhile, as in all societies of conquerors and conquered, human nature prevailed, and despite all the social difficulties involved, intermarriage occurred and blurred the lines between the two peoples.

In Wales as in England, a number of prosperous new men were building up estates. They were not noble, but they were, economically, part of the upper class. This group, known as the gentry or the country gentlemen or the squires, is unique to Britain. In other European nations they would have been incorporated as lesser aristocrats. In England and Wales they remained commoners at law. In fact, country gentlemen could compose most of the membership in the House of Commons because of their legal status as non-noble commoners. Outside of that, there was nothing at all common about them. Numerically they were a very tiny part of the population of Wales, just 2 or 3 percent, but they were enormously influential in the countryside. They were the Welsh most connected with English culture and language, the people most likely to petition to be "made English."

In the towns, merchants and tradesmen prospered and became members of their governing corporations as burgesses. The woolen and woolen cloth trade became increasingly important. Even so, the overwhelming majority of Welsh people were rural, just as they had always been. Only a small percentage of the population, certainly fewer than 10 percent, lived in towns and, by modern standards, nearly all of these towns would be called villages today.

The countryside took some time to recover from the effects of widespread pillaging, devastation and depopulation from the rebellion. Nevertheless, by the late 15th century there was an increase in prosperity. With fewer people on the land, reflecting not only the rebellion but also the long-term effects of the 14th century black plague, wages were higher. Population totals moved upwards once more. By the early 16th century it would be estimated at just over a quarter of a million.

After the Edwardian conquest Wales became an important recruiting ground for soldiers to serve English kings. Wales was noted for its bowmen and spearmen who came from all over the principality. For 800 years thereafter England's wars would also be Wales' wars. In later centuries Scotland and Ireland would also contribute mightily to English arms.

The Welsh were particularly prominent in the Hundred Years' War, which took place between 1337 and 1453, and consisted of a series of attempts by the English crown to assert its claim to France. While the English won most of the spectacular battles, they eventually lost the war. It is estimated that at one of the most famous battles, Crécy, one third of the English army was actually Welsh. The Welsh were also exceptionally conspicuous in the ranks at the famous victory at Agincourt, the battle celebrated in Shakespeare's *Henry V*. In addition, many prominent Welshmen served as officers. One of them, however, Owain Lawgoch, fought for the French.

One of the more unfortunate aspects of this ongoing struggle against France was that Wales, like England, periodically became home to many unruly demobilized soldiers. Outbursts of lawlessness can also be attributed to some former followers of Owen Glendower who remained in the hills as outlaws.

England replaced France and Scotland as the field for the deployment of Welsh mercenaries in the late 15th

The Battle of Agincourt in 1415, one of Henry V's great victories in France, all of them won with the help of Welsh soldiers.

century as the descendants of the Plantagenet dynasty of England struggled to gain the English throne, aided and abetted by rival factions of powerful nobles. These struggles, lasting from 1455 to 1485, were called the Wars of the Roses. The two Houses, Lancaster and York, fought all over England. Marcher lords fought on each side, usually on battlefields in England. The date that these struggles terminated has been noted as one of the hallmarks of the end of the Middle Ages.

Historians have long debated when the Middle Ages actually came to an end. Various dates have been chosen, all of them clustering around the year 1500. Americans prefer to use 1492, the year of Columbus' discovery; Germans prefer 1517, the date when Martin Luther dramatically challenged the universal church in the West. The English and Welsh are likely to cite 1485, the year when the Tudor dynasty came to power. All of these dates point to major changes in the pattern of medieval life in all of the more advanced parts of Europe: the discovery of a new world overseas, the break with the universal church and the establishment of strong, modernizing, unifying monarchies that sought to curb powerful subjects and the remnants of feudalism. There were other new worlds to discover — that of the telescope and the microscope, and a classical old world, that of the Greeks and Romans, to rediscover. This fresh burst of creativity was called the Renaissance and it would take almost two hundred years before northern Europe, including the island of Britain, enjoyed its own version of it.

Since Wales was overwhelmingly rural and still rather remote, these changes had little impact at first. But 1485 was nonetheless an extremely significant date for Welsh history. The Tudor dynasty originated in Wales, and its first ruler, Henry VII, was claimed by the Welsh as the long-sought heir to King Arthur, the king who would save Wales from oppression.

Henry VII, A Welsh Hero — 1485 to 1509

The very first monarch of the Tudor dynasty was probably the most able ruler England ever had. His children, Henry VIII, Bloody Mary and Elizabeth I, enjoy more worldwide fame than any other monarchs who ever ruled in England. Yet their father, the founder of the dynasty, Henry VII, is much more of an obscure figure in history. He was certainly not glamorous, but he may have been the most intelligent and politically adept member of this outstanding dynasty.

He won his crown on the battlefield as a Lancastrian candidate in one of the many contests near the end of the Wars of the Roses. He embarked upon his campaign from Wales with a rather weak hereditary claim and a small army of adventurers. Family branch extinctions and military fortunes made his weak claim to the throne possible. When his reign ended decades later, his throne was secure, he had a legitimate male heir, England and Wales were at peace and his treasury was full. No one dared to rival his son, Henry VIII. Considering the odds against him at the outset, he had an outstandingly successful life.

His Welsh origin is significant. He was the scion of a marcher family established in the Welsh city of Pembroke, his birthplace. His grandfather was a mere Welsh gentleman, Owain or Owen Tudor, who served in the army of the dashing English king, Henry V. A famous Shakespeare play named after this king celebrates his heroic campaigns in France. After Henry V died, Owain served in the household of the king's widow, Catherine of Valois. Around 1432, Owain's fortune was substantially improved by secretly wooing and marrying his royal employer. The English court was highly displeased at the queen dowager's seduction by someone so far beneath her status and launched an inquiry. The couple remained steadfast, however, and produced two sons, one of whom, Edmund, the Earl of Richmond, was the future Henry VII's father. His mother was the remarkable, well educated and high born Elizabeth Beaufort, another royal descendant, but from an illegitimate line. The other son, Jasper Tudor, the Earl of Pembroke, Henry VII's uncle, became the standard bearer of the House of Lancaster despite the fact that his thin royal blood came only from his mother and not from Owain, his father. Owain himself was a casualty of the bloody struggles for the throne. He was beheaded by Edward VI after being taken prisoner at the Battle of Mortimer's Cross in 1461.

Henry was Edmund's posthumous son who was taken under the protection of Jasper. His uncle took him to a wise exile in France while the Wars of the Roses raged and various claimants were destroyed, including two little princes murdered in the Tower of London. Their uncle, Richard III, who was made forever sinister by Shakespeare, took the throne for the House of York. At this juncture, the Tudors decided to take a desperate gamble. Henry, aged 20, set sail from France with a fleet under his uncle Jasper's command. The army contained

Henry VII, the first of the Tudor Dynasty from Wales.

400 Lancastrian exiles, a French force and a Scottish company. It landed in southwestern Wales at Milford Haven and marched up and across Wales to the Welsh border, flying the banner of the Welsh red dragon, building up support and drawing recruits from the Welsh countryside. Henry promised to restore the Welsh to their liberties and free them from the "miserable servitudes" that had been imposed upon them through the penal laws.

His outnumbered force eventually met the army of king Richard III at the Battle of Bosworth in 1485. One contingent of Richard's army held back, and in a furious battle the Lancastrians defeated the Yorkists. Richard himself was slain on the battlefield. Shakespeare depicted him losing his mount and running about on foot, sword in hand, shouting that now famous phrase: "A horse, a horse, my kingdom for a horse!"

Henry VII ruled brilliantly from the start. He began by dating his reign on the day before Bosworth, so that he could confiscate all the lands of his enemies for treason. He collected taxes carefully and guarded the royal treasury throughout his reign, knowing instinctively that money meant power. He also foiled the plots of his rivals and brought peace and order to the realm by using the judicial system forcefully. The unruly nobility had heavy fines imposed upon them for violence.

Both he and his subjects yearned for the end of baronial strife. Henry, who had been through fierce military campaigns to stay alive and gain his throne, had no desire to engage in costly war. His hard life in exile taught him to be a fine judge of people, so his choice of administrators was excellent. He also filled the then depleted ranks of the nobility with new nobles likely to be stalwart defenders of the Tudor dynasty.

For the Welsh, Henry VII was a true Welshman, the heir to Owen Glendower, the king who would not only unify Wales but who would make Wales, the home of the true Britons, supreme over England. In actuality, Henry VII was only one-quarter Welsh, a heritage from his grandfather, Owain Tudor. He was also one-quarter French and half English. Nevertheless, he emphasized his Welshness to unify Wales and England. Since he had a weak hereditary claim, he could connect himself through his Welsh ancestry to ancient British kings who ruled before the coming of the Normans and the Plantagenets. It is not surprising that he named his first born son Arthur, after the most famous of the ancient British kings. Arthur became a very significant Prince of Wales as his father revived the importance of that position. Arthur died before he ever came to the throne and Henry VII was eventually succeeded by his second son, the famous Henry VIII.

A shrewd ruler, Henry VII emphasized his ancestry in Wales more so than he did in England, where he needed to emphasize his shaky claim to descend from English royal lines. Even so, he added the Welsh red dragon to England's royal arms and the Welsh griffin to his badge. Some Welsh found more concrete advantages from having a king with a Welsh background: many Welsh bishops and civil administrators were appointed. Welsh families such as the Cecils, known for producing several famous crown ministers in later centuries, received royal patronage and advancement in English society. Meanwhile, an increasing number of ambitious Welsh with less claim to patronage

The tower at Pembroke Castle in which Henry VII was born.

made their way to London to find their fortunes, a theme that has recurred to the present day.

Wales was peaceful under the Tudors. Like other strong monarchs in early modern times, the Tudors executed mighty subjects who were suspected of treason. What made the Tudors so effective is that they were, with the exception of Mary I, very skillful in applying the executioner's ax. Therefore marcher lords were restrained from disloyal behavior by the occasional sudden departure of one of their colleagues. Gradually, the marcher lordships were absorbed by the crown. Meanwhile the Tudors arranged marriages between the families of marcher lords and people related to their dynasty in order to shore up support.

Henry VII preferred to rule Wales through a new body called the Council of Wales and the Marches, brought into existence in Shropshire 1501. Its ostensible purpose was to enforce law and order in border areas and to prevent lawbreakers from escaping punishment by fleeing from one march to another. It was under Prince Arthur and dominated by English administrators. As time went on, more and more Welsh administrators would sit on it. It lasted until the end of the 17th century. Despite its initial English composition, it nevertheless put a clear political focus on all of Wales and strove for greater unity and control.

The Council of Wales had a Lord President, a deputy and 22 members, all of whom were royal nominees. It served both as a court of appeal and as a supervisory administrative body. It was responsible for implementing the Acts of Parliament and appointing shire officials, including sheriffs and Justices of the Peace.

The Council of Wales was but one aspect of Henry VII's efforts to consolidate his rule throughout his realm, a pattern followed by many European monarchs around that time. To an extent it brought greater crown control and uniformity to Wales, but overall his advances in Wales were piecemeal, gradual and of limited effectiveness. Radical consolidation in the form of annexation came in the reign of his son.

The Chapel of Henry VII in Westminster Abbey, showing some Welsh heraldry.

Henry VIII and Unification with England — 1509 to 1603

Everyone knows something about Henry VIII, celebrated for his six wives and the demise of two of them via the royal executioner. He was a colorful figure. In his youth he was brilliant, accomplished, good natured and admired by all. As he got older, this man of great appetite became more sour and despotic, dominating Parliament and laying the charge of treason upon those who disagreed with him.

While popular interest in his reign has centered around his remarkably charismatic personality, a Tudor revolution in government, designed to centralize and modernize, was being accomplished by his royal council. The drive to create a more centralized, controlled and efficient monarchy, begun under his father, culminated in a series of major changes in church and state during Henry VIII's reign. These developments had a profound impact upon Wales.

To carry out major changes, Henry VIII, like his father, brought new, able, efficient and well-educated men into his inner councils, many of them middle-class men, born outside of the traditional ruling class, the nobility. They investigated key aspects of his realm, provided reports based on the facts they gathered and drafted statutes to bring about change. This was the beginning of modern bureaucratic procedures in England. The statutes were presented to Parliament, where loyalty to Henry's wishes was taken for granted and enforced by fear. It was said that Henry VIII ruled his Parliaments through an iron fist in a velvet glove. Parliament served to amplify his voice, to declare that whatever the king wished was actually the will of the whole realm, king, lords and commons united.

Wales was the recipient of one of the most significant pieces of Henry VIII's legislation, the Act of Union of 1536. What it did was amalgamate England and Wales, abolish the marches and establish a uniform administrative structure. Another act of union in 1543 bolstered the original statute. According to the language of the Act of Union, Wales and England were to be one indissoluble kingdom. Wales was to be "incorporated, annexed, united and subject" to the English crown. Ironically, an English dynasty with Welsh roots brought an end to Wales as a separate, anomalous political entity.

Specifically, the Act of Union declared that all officials in Wales were to be English speaking and all legal proceedings were to be in English. Various "sinister usages and customs" in Wales were to be eliminated. This meant, among other things, the end of the Welsh inheritance practice of dividing up lands among multiple heirs. Henceforth, lands could be held together "after the English tenure without division or partition." The Welsh were to "enjoy and inherit" as Englishmen. This meant that Welsh gentlemen were allowed to preserve their family estates by passing them on to one male heir, a practice called primogeniture. English estates had been built up over the centuries through primogeniture.

All of Wales was divided up into shires, including the marcher lordships. All the Welsh were to be equal before the law. This meant that the anti-Welsh penal legislation was superseded. These glaring statutes from the time of Owen Glendower's rebellion had become a dead letter under the Tudors anyway. English civil law joined English criminal law to prevail everywhere, eliminating the last vestiges of old Welsh law.

The whole apparatus of English local government was to operate in Wales also, meaning that sheriffs, Justices of the Peace, coroners and shire courts would function everywhere. If any Welshman wanted to participate in this governing structure, he would have to speak English, because that was to be the only language of law and administration. Henry's ministers saw the English language as an instrument to amalgamate Wales in a unified, centralized kingdom.

Wales gained representation in the English Parliament, but of a somewhat different nature than that of England. Each shire in Wales was to have one Member of Parliament, while English shires had two. Welsh boroughs, or towns, were grouped together in each shire for the purpose of sending only one burgess to Parliament to represent all of the boroughs. In England, each and every incorporated borough sent two members. In sum, Wales gained only 26 Members of Parliament out of the grand total of 349 members. This looks like flagrant under-representation but Wales had only around 275,000 people at the time of the Act of Union and England had 3.75 million. So Wales had roughly 7 percent of the English population and roughly 7 percent of the Members of Parliament. Having only one member for each shire's boroughs and one member for each shire really reflected the thinly populated nature of Wales.

An idealization of the 17th century English country gentleman, a type copied widely by Welsh gentlemen.

The effects of the Acts of Union have remained controversial in Welsh history. The Welsh gentry and merchant class, a small minority of the population, generally welcomed this legislation. It gave them equality before the law and offered them many opportunities to advance, either as local Justices of the Peace or as emigrants to London. A large number of ambitious Welshmen did go to London in Tudor times to seek their fortunes as lawyers, craftsmen, shopkeepers and merchants. Those who remained in Wales were able to enjoy a more stable, more lawful environment as a stronger administration of the law was applied. Now the Welsh gentry could build up their estates in tranquility and gain control over local affairs by sitting on the bench as Justices of the Peace.

The negative side involved the proscription of the Welsh language for any official purposes, and the end of old Welsh law which had operated in community life for centuries. Above all, a greater division was created between the very small upper class of Wales and the Welsh masses below. The gentry were most interested in expanding their estates and taking up English ways. Many of the more ambitious of the middle classes also took to anglicization, a word that means becoming more English. Meanwhile, the local small farmers, laborers and ordinary craftsmen were left behind in relative poverty, and the cultural and economic gap between them and the small minority at the top continued to grow. Ordinary people continued to speak Welsh and carry on with Welsh customs, thereby preserving the ancient culture at the grass roots level.

Scotland and Ireland had Acts of Union also, at the beginning of the 18th century for Scotland and at the beginning of the 19th century for Ireland. Yet there was a fundamental difference between these amalgamations and that of Wales. Scotland and Ireland had their own Parliaments, and the English government had to bribe and coerce its members wholesale to get them to vote for union. No matter how corrupt these actions were, the Scots and the Irish who were represented in their Parliaments had at least some institutional bargaining power to gain the best arrangement for themselves. The Welsh had no such opportunity. Their union was pushed through unilaterally without negotiations or representation.

Because union with England had come centuries earlier for Wales than it did for Scotland and Ireland, there was no chance for Welsh national institutions to develop. Therefore the only vehicle remaining to preserve the values, symbols and myths of Welsh nationality was the Welsh language. Increasingly, those at the top of Welsh society abandoned it, but those below maintained it to the present day.

The Reformation in Wales Under Henry VIII and Elizabeth I

Another important change that Henry VIII imposed on his realm was his break with the Roman Catholic Church. The floodgates of the Reformation were opened in England not by any theological stand, as in Germany under the influence of Martin Luther or western Europe under the influence of John Calvin. Henry VIII broke with Rome from 1527 to 1539 initially because of personal and dynastic reasons. He needed a legitimate male heir to continue the Tudor line and the Catholic Church would not grant him a timely annulment from his marriage to Catherine of Aragon so that he could marry the pregnant Anne Boleyn, his mistress. The Anglican Church, or the Church of England, arose from that rather sordid circumstance. Henry VIII was proclaimed Head of the Church of England, replacing the Pope in that role. A church court in England then became responsible for adjudicating his marital problem rather than a foreign church court.

The quick results of adjudication were favorable to the king's suit, of course, and the path was cleared for a hasty marriage to Anne Boleyn. The supposed male heir in her womb turned out to be a daughter. Henry should not have been disappointed, however, because that daughter, when she became Elizabeth I, turned out to be the most successful and most celebrated of all the monarchs in English history.

The new Anglican Church had many offshoots eventually, including The Church of Ireland and the Church of Wales. When the United States became independent of Britain centuries later, the American version of the Anglican Church became the Episcopal Church. They all drew their worship from the new Prayer Books of the Church of England, which spelt out rituals, in English, which were largely based on the old Latin rituals of the historic Roman Catholic Church. Meanwhile, Roman Catholics continued to maintain that there was only one universal Christian Church. Catholics therefore spoke of their Church "in" various places rather than "of" various places, a situation liable to lead to confusion. The various European churches that broke from Rome were given the collective designation "Protestant" because they protested against the universal authority of Rome and various Catholic practices.

In the future Wales would be noted for its staunch Protestantism, but in the reign of Henry VIII, the Welsh were passive over the break with Rome. The Welsh people did not participate actively to help bring about the Reformation. They accepted the changes without enthusiasm or did not know about them. In effect, they and their English neighbors went to bed as Roman Catholics one night and as Anglicans the next night.

The Reformation in England was actually an act of state carried out by legislation passed in Parliament. Every act that set up the new church was completely prepared for the Members of Parliament by the royal council and pushed through without opposition. Henry VIII's Parliaments were carefully chosen and served him well in

Henry the VIII, who brought the Reformation to Wales.

proclaiming a national endorsement of his will. That is why he called them in the first place. Nevertheless, in the long run, Henry's rigged Parliaments were beneficial for constitutional development because that old, Medieval institution was placed at the center of affairs and that gave it new, modern life.

Welshmen and Englishmen did not notice very many Protestant changes at first. The same buildings, personnel and generally similar rituals were used as before. But one striking change was the use of the English language instead of Latin. In Wales, the Reformation was hardly implemented in remote areas and rituals continued as before. Major changes would come later on, when the Prayer Book and Bible were translated into Welsh.

The most notable Protestant innovation in England and Wales was the destruction of monasteries, abbeys and convents, religious houses that were deemed no longer useful for society. Henry closed them all, pensioning off the religious persons who cooperated and executing the few monks who resisted or who refused to swear allegiance to his new position. In Wales only two clergymen refused and thereby became Roman Catholic martyrs. In England a small number also refused, the most famous of whom was Sir Thomas More, who became the Roman Catholics' martyr Saint Thomas More as a result.

These confiscated religious houses came with a considerable amount of land. Henry sold the land off rather cheaply to enrich the crown. The landed classes of England and Wales, particularly the rising gentry class, were able to add to their holdings at bargain prices and at the expense of the church. This gave them a strong economic incentive to support what became known as the Henrician Reformation.

Wales had around fifty religious houses and the surrounding gentry were happy to take over their lands on very favorable terms. Monastic buildings were looted, stripped of their lead roofs and even used as stone quarries. Wales today has several striking ruins from the time of Henry VIII. Tintern Abbey is famous, enduringly beautiful in its stripped, pillaged state.

When Henry VIII died in 1547, church doctrine remained unsettled. A new force in Protestantism, called Puritanism, pushed for greater change in the Anglican

Tintern Abbey in Monmouthshire, one of the famous ruins left by Henry VIII's Reformation.

Church to make it more Protestant and less like the Roman Catholic Church. Puritans were inspired by the French theologian John Calvin who sought to "purify" the Church by basing it strictly on the Bible and emphasizing sermons based upon Scripture. Churches were to be more plain and simple, rituals reduced, and society reformed according to their interpretation of God's will.

Before the Puritans could agitate for change in Elizabeth's reign, they had to suffer persecution under her elder sister Queen Mary I, Henry VIII's Roman Catholic daughter. She is known in history as "Bloody Mary" because she burned Anglican Protestant martyrs. Only three of them were Welsh. At this time Protestantism tended to be supported by people living in urban communities and Wales remained overwhelmingly rural and Welsh speaking. This shut Wales out of the feverish theological developments going on in England for a time.

This situation changed dramatically under Elizabeth I who reigned from 1558 to 1603. An Act of Parliament of 1563 ordered bishops in Wales to provide Welsh translations of the New Testament and Book of Common Prayer. By 1567 copies were to be in every church in Wales. The whole Bible in translation was prepared by 1588 and similarly distributed. These translations went far beyond merely bolstering the Anglican Church in Wales. Through them a sense of national identity was maintained. Welsh became the official language of public worship and religious life and thereby served to sustain the ancient culture in modern times. So, despite the loss of a separate political status in the early 16th century, the translation of the Bible into Welsh preserved the Welsh culture permanently.

These translations also eventually led to staunch Protestantism as a foundation of Welsh communities in modern times. Wales accepted the Reformation and did not suffer the fate of Ireland, where Catholicism remained entrenched because the Irish were not provided with a Bible in Irish until long after the Reformation crisis was over. This is yet another example of how vital the Welsh language has been in Welsh history.

A Welsh bishop and Cambridge graduate named William Morgan (1545–1604) initially translated the Bible into Welsh. His work has been regarded as exceptionally accurate and very sensitive in utilizing the beauty and strength of the language. William Salesbury, an Oxford-educated literary lawyer, translated the Prayerbook and provided the earliest translation of the New Testament.

Elizabeth fostered these translations for the benefit of the Anglican Church in Wales and they succeeded beyond expectations. Elizabeth herself was a moderate Anglican who followed a course right down the middle between the more extreme Protestants on the one hand, or to her left, and the remaining Roman Catholics on the other, or her right. Most Welsh found her moderate Anglicanism quite suitable. Some Welsh in remote areas continued to carry on the old Catholic practices. Images, relics, holy wells and shrines, all proscribed by Protestants, had always been important in rural Wales.

On the opposite side of the religious spectrum, some Welsh scholars educated in "new learning" did embrace Puritanism heartily. Elizabeth regarded Puritans as treasonous if they agitated for radical changes in the Anglican Church and she put the worst offenders to death. One of them was John Penry, a Welshman educated at both Cambridge and Oxford. He was the first Welsh Puritan martyr, following the path of the three Welsh Anglican martyrs executed by Elizabeth's sister, Mary I.

Religious changes in England and Wales coincided with a decided economic upswing in Tudor times. A better-fed population grew, trade expanded and estates grew in size and prosperity. This economic advance was much more notable in England than in Wales. Most of Wales remained essentially pastoral because of difficult terrain, soil and climate. Sheep did well in Welsh hills, and good land along the coasts could yield harvests of wheat and barley.

Some very small extractive industries operated in Tudor times: some copper was mined from scattered locations and some coal was dug from seams near the earth's surface. Coal, which became so vital to the Welsh economy in modern times, was already being exported to Ireland, England and France during Elizabeth's reign. Even so, Welsh industry was still rudimentary compared to the huge concentrations that would be established later.

The population in the early reign of Henry VIII was approximately only a quarter of a million. It would grow to about 360,000 in 1620. Life remained hard and short for most Welsh people regardless of the Tudor economic surge. Most communities were remote and given over to continuing with old ways.

At the bottom of Welsh society were impoverished agricultural laborers, and just above them husbandmen living off the land close to the subsistence level. Wales also had its share of paupers and vagrants, made destitute by various misfortunes of life. Some more prosperous yeomen farmers were higher in the social scale. Most of these ordinary Welsh people hardly ever left their native villages and then they did not travel very far. Of course, Welsh soldiers, sailors and merchants got out into the wider world.

Only 2 or 3 percent of the Welsh population lived lives of comfort and privilege, the wealthiest of them living on large estates, inhabiting grand houses, where they employed numerous servants. They were prosperous Welsh gentry. They made education, particularly legal studies, one of their vital interests. One college at Oxford, Jesus College, founded in 1571, was based on a gift from an important family in Wales. Jesus College became the college noted for educating Welsh gentlemen and clerics. Others went to Cambridge or the Inns of Court in London where they studied law. Some children of the gentry went to English schools or English grammar schools founded in Wales. There they studied the classics of Greece and Rome and became more anglicized in the process.

The gentry of Wales dominated local society until the 19th century. They took a keen interest in English law and controlled the administration of local justice. The size and prosperity of their estates was absolutely crucial to maintain their lavish standard of living. Since Tudor times were inflationary, they had to increase their holdings, and they often did so at the expense of the poor. The Welsh gentry often tried to pay the lowest wages possible and enclose the open common land that the village people had used for centuries to eke out an existence. The decay of manorialism and the dissolution of the monasteries gave them many opportunities to snatch up additional land advantageously. Even with all of these procedures, Wales continued to be known in England for its relatively less well off gentry.

The gentry had a penchant for genealogy and strove to display impressive family trees and pedigrees, regardless of how dubious they may have been. Their status as a thin ruling crust in Welsh society was condoned by the masses because in these centuries the hierarchical order of society was almost uniformly accepted as natural. From a common person's point of view, God in His wisdom had had created ranks for the better ordering of society. After all, Heaven itself had its hierarchy.

The specially privileged lives of the Welsh gentry in early modern times brought a new division to Wales. The gentry were highly anglicized, usually abandoning the Welsh language and taking up the latest English ways. They worked with the English government and in the English economic system. Some of them did not abandon Welsh culture, but, in general, it was the ordinary people beneath them who retained the Welsh culture in early modern times. They were mostly illiterate rural folk living modest lives.

Elizabeth's reign saw the flowering of the Renaissance in Britain. The most well known name of all the island's great Renaissance artists was, of course, William Shakespeare, who did have some kind of Welsh connection. Various Welsh characters appeared in his popular plays, including buffoons, patriots, ladies and gentlemen. Who can forget Fluellen, which is a corruption of Llywelyn, a vain, quarrelsome Welsh patriot who was a very capable soldier? Or Lady Mortimer, a softhearted, gentle Welsh lady who found English pronunciations difficult? The line:

"Eat thy leek, thou knave!" is immortal. These Welsh characters delighted his audiences then and they continue to do so in the new millennium.

Just where did Shakespeare learn to seize upon Welsh stereotypes so brilliantly? This question, like so many about the Bard of Avon, remains shrouded in mystery. Perhaps he observed the Welsh in their populous London colony or perhaps he knew the Welsh drovers and others that went through Stratford upon Avon on their way to England's metropolis. Some go so far as to contend that William Shakespeare must have been Welsh himself!

Wales Under the Stuarts and Cromwell — 1603 to 1714

English history in the 17th century is more complex and difficult to comprehend than Welsh history. Wales was not a center for the tumultuous events of these years. The Stuart dynasty, which sought to rule England from 1603 to 1714, experienced two civil wars; the growth of revolutionary ideologies; a republic under a military dictator, Oliver Cromwell; a restoration of the monarchy; and yet another revolution followed by another dynastic change.

What happened in Wales was much less complicated. At the beginning of the Stuart era, Wales was still a poor, undeveloped area with a small middle class. Well into the Stuart era, in 1670, the population of Wales was estimated to be only 370,000, of whom five out of six were rural dwellers. In the 17th century, support for new, radical ideas stressing opposition to the crown came from an environment that Wales lacked: a large urban milieu possessing substantial numbers from the professional and merchant classes. Therefore, through most of the 17th century nearly all of Wales was royalist, supporting the crown against the rebellious Parliament.

The Welsh gentry welcomed the first Stuart king, James I, and were rewarded with offices, honors and various favors in return. While many in Wales were unhappy with the policies of his son, Charles I, who raised taxes throughout his kingdom by rather arbitrary means, Wales remained loyal. After a time England's Parliament rebelled against him and the king raised an army to fight Parliamentary forces. Wales supported the monarch, as did so many of the English living in rural counties in the north and west of Britain.

Undoubtedly most Welsh were indifferent to the struggles looming in England, but the strategic location of Wales forced their participation in the first English Civil War. Key routes to ports in northern and southern Wales linked the king's headquarters in southern England with his loyal supporters in Ireland. Moreover, Wales became an important recruiting ground for troops, and was mentioned as "the nursery of the king's infantry." Some great landowners in Wales conscripted their tenants for military service for the king. Wales was also a refuge when the king had to retreat from southern England.

In a very few places, south Pembrokeshire in particular, towns and local gentry supported the Parliamentary side and joined forces that cut the royal roads to Ireland. Royalists with Irish reinforcements reopened them. Elsewhere castles held out for the royalist side and fell one after another as the Parliamentary side triumphed. Of course, these campaigns were on a small scale. The outcome of the civil war was decided by the major campaigns and battles in England.

Defeated and desperate, King Charles I mustered a new force drawn, in part, from some of his former enemies. In a second civil war he was defeated again, and this time the radical faction in charge in Parliament and in the army

The scenic Pembrokeshire Coast.

put the king on trial and executed him. Among those who signed the king's death warrant were two Welshmen.

For a time England and Wales were controlled by a republican form of government, called at first the Commonwealth and then the Protectorate. In effect it was a military dictatorship under Oliver Cromwell, a reluctant dictator. One of Cromwell's many victorious campaigns in the civil wars had been in Wales. When he was installed in power he governed Wales and England directly, without the Council of Wales. He temporarily abolished it, along with the English House of Lords and the Established Church in England and Wales. Ireland and Scotland still remained as separate entities. Many royalists in all of Cromwell's domains had to pay heavy fines and many had their estates confiscated. In Wales as elsewhere, new men bought up these lands cheaply and became new gentry families.

What gave the Parliamentary side the ideological strength to fight and destroy the monarchy was a new religious faith known to history as Puritanism. It was from this English Puritan impulse of the 17th century that the famous Welsh religious life of later centuries originated. While there were always some Puritans in Wales from the onset of the movement, the Puritan impulse did not sweep the principality until the 18th century.

At the beginning of the 17th century, Puritans agitated for change within the Established Church. By the end of the 17th century, they had divided among themselves and formed several separate denominations outside of the Established Church, including Baptists, Congregationalists, Presbyterians and Quakers. All of these new Puritan denominations refused to conform to the rituals of the Anglican Church, which was reestablished in 1660, and so they gained the collective name of "Nonconformists." They were also called "Dissenters" because they dissented from the Anglican Church.

Puritans were Bible-based Protestants who were inspired by the French theologian, John Calvin, who sought to "purify" the Anglican Church by making it more Protestant and less Catholic. This meant eliminating abuses and emphasizing sermons and the Bible more than ritual. Puritan churches were plain and simple. Puritans felt they were doing God's will, and would carry on with zeal at any cost. They saw themselves as a spiritual elite predestined for salvation, activists who were God's instruments in a fallen world. There was also a democratic impulse in Puritanism. In their congregations, all believers were equal. They had no bishops and their ministers were ordinary people.

During the 17th century and the civil wars, most people in Wales continued to embrace the Anglican Church enthusiastically. The Puritans made strong efforts to bring the Welsh over to their new faith, including traveling preachers and free public schools for both sexes. Puritan ministers were appointed to many Welsh parishes, in what they called "the dark corners of the land." These were seeds for the future, but Puritanism would only take hold much later on, when urban life was more developed.

To be sure, the Established Church in Wales, the Anglican Church, did have its share of abuses before the Puritans arrived. There were too few preachers and occasional neglect of pastoral duties, such as visiting the sick, baptism and burial. Some clergy held several church positions at the same time and were non-residents in them, turning over their responsibilities to ill-paid subordinates. Moreover, many of the Welsh appointments fell to Englishmen. During the time that the Puritans ruled England, hundreds of Welsh clergymen were ejected from their positions and replaced. The charges ranged from drunkenness to supporting royal pretensions.

Nevertheless, Anglicans maintained their practices defiantly in England and Wales during the Puritan revolution. Once Cromwell was in his grave Puritan rule crumbled. The Anglican Church was reestablished in England

Oliver Cromwell, the Puritan dictator who led a campaign to crush royalist forces in Wales.

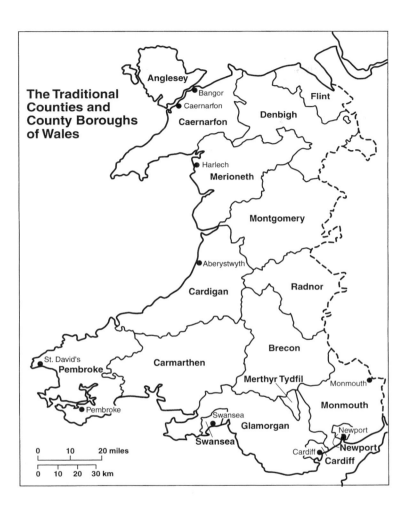

The Traditional
Counties and
County Boroughs
of Wales

Anglesey

Bangor
Caernarfon
Caernarfon

Flint

Denbigh

Harlech

Merioneth

Montgomery

Aberystwyth

Cardigan

Radnor

Brecon

St. David's
Pembroke

Carmarthen

Merthyr Tydfil

Monmouth

Pembroke

Monmouth

Swansea
Swansea

Glamorgan

Newport
Newport

Cardiff
Cardiff

0	10	20 miles

0	10	20	30 km

and Wales along with the restored Stuart dynasty in 1660. Then it was the turn of the new Puritan ministers in Wales and elsewhere to be forced out of their parishes. Reliable Anglicans replaced them.

The Welsh were generally relieved to see the end of experimentation in church and state and to return to what they saw as normal. Many old royalists returned to their lands as restrictions were put on Puritan worship and the Puritan schools were disbanded. It is estimated that with all their efforts, the Puritans were only able to convert 5 percent of the Welsh population. In south Wales, where there was more commerce, more schools and Anglicized towns, the figure may have been as high as 10 percent. This percentage would grow enormously in the next centuries.

The restored Anglicans certainly wanted to keep the Puritans from ever becoming a political force in Britain again. Therefore they imposed political discrimination under the Test Act, which was not repealed until 1828. The Test Act sought to reserve public office holding to Anglicans. Nevertheless, Puritans gained protection for worship and private religious life by the Toleration Act of 1689. This major step forward in civil rights meant that the old punishments for not conforming to the Established Church ended.

For most of Wales, the local Anglican squire and the local Anglican parson were still the dominant figures that local people usually both respected and feared. Rank, titles and birth remained important to those who led Welsh society, the gentry and nobility. In the late 17th century they built great mansions and were divided from ordinary Welsh people by a huge difference in wealth and a growing difference in language. The upper, landed classes increasingly spoke English exclusively, took up English customs and copied current English fashions.

Far below them, Welsh yeomen were reasonably well-off, sometimes sending their sons to schools and serving as local parish officials. Agricultural pursuits and craftsmanship were not strictly divided. Many Welsh agricultural workers developed one or another craft skill while many craftsmen ran some livestock. Beneath them was a large force of mobile agricultural workers who did not own land. They were relatively unskilled and worked for long hours for pathetic wages.

The poor were always vulnerable. Physical or mental illness, old age, disabilities or bad harvests could thrust them into misery and dependence upon the rudimentary welfare system of their own parish. They were out of luck for assistance if they were not living in their native parish or could not be sent back to it. In the Stuart era, a distinction was drawn between the "deserving" poor and the "undeserving" poor. Vagabonds, vagrants and known rogues were undeserving. They were arrested, physically punished and sent off to their native parishes.

Despite the vast maldistribution of wealth in Wales, the lower orders generally acquiesced in rule by an increasingly anglicized upper class. Division of society into the high and low was seen as part of the divine plan for human communities. Radical opposition to this point of view would not develop in Wales for another century or century and a half. Wales remained a particularly conservative, quiet part of Great Britain, strongly royalist and strongly Anglican. Wales regularly returned conservative Tory Members of Parliament until the middle of the 18th century.

The 17th and early 18th centuries were less peaceful for the other two parts of England's so-called "internal empire," Ireland and Scotland. After the Battle of the Boyne in 1690, which is still celebrated by marching Protestant Orangemen every July, the Catholic majority was put under a severe Penal Code which forced them into submission to a ruling Protestant elite. Scotland was joined with England in an Act of Union in 1707 which was followed by two bloody rebellions and a brutal suppression of Scottish culture that went so far as to ban tartans and bagpipes. By contrast, Wales glided into the 18th century calmly.

Wales in the 18th Century

The most important developments in Wales in the 18th century were religious and educational rather than political. In this century, a powerful Christian Evangelical movement swept through Wales and transformed Welsh society for all time. It marked the full flowering of the impulses of the Reformation and of Puritan Protestantism in Wales. It brought with it a campaign against illiteracy and for mass education. It warred upon drunkenness, profanity and the remaining pagan feasts and festivals.

The Methodists led the way down the path of evangelical ardor, soon to be followed by the various Nonconformist Churches. Methodism was not one of the old Puritan sects, but an 18th century offshoot of Anglicanism stressing a more intense and personal religious life. The Methodists were often known as Wesleyans, a name derived from one of the movement's English founders, John Wesley.

The Methodists began as pious Anglicans who met together in classes and preached with great drama, emotion and enthusiasm. Provocative preaching was carried on out of doors and in private homes as well as in church. Methodist preachers would show up at such places as market places and fairs. Inspired by fiery preaching, a network of small, devout groups quickly spread. Conversion in these groups was intensely personal. Methodists bared their souls to each other, confessing their sins, expressing their fears, and relating the joys of their own personal conversions. The progress of each member of their small classes of half-a-dozen to a dozen was important and carefully observed. The Methodists gave to their adherents what successful religious, social or political groups and cults provide: a sense of belonging by giving the individual a secure emotional home within the group.

Methodism in several variants suited the ordinary Welsh admirably. It was more plain and simple than Anglicanism, stressing prayer and the Bible rather than ritual. It maintained an atmosphere of equality, rejecting an official hierarchy and incorporating local people in positions of church leadership.

The spirited and melodic hymns of the Methodists increased religious fervor and joyfulness. The joining of famous Methodist hymns with the Welsh language has been called one of the greatest art forms of British civilization. Methodist choirs and schools in Wales became the greatest single repository and forum of Welsh culture and contributed immensely to its revival and to the survival of the Welsh language.

The Methodists also emphasized education. Sunday schools were for both children and adults. Learning to read was important because the individual could then read the Bible which was published in Welsh in large quantities along with other religious material. The growth of literacy in Wales and in the Welsh language was a highly significant development. Through all of these efforts, the Methodists became utterly convinced that they were doing

God's work by fulfilling His plan to transform Wales into a truly Christian society.

Methodism in Wales tended to be different in some ways from Methodism in England. It was more Calvinistic, meaning that it was more connected to the strict theology of grace and outlook on life that had so influenced the Puritans of the 17th century. Puritan virtues of honesty, thrift and temperance were to the forefront. Given the fact that Wales did not have the diverse cultural life of English cities, the chapel soon became one of the main social centers for Welsh people. The Welsh Methodists have been criticized for being too narrow and pietistic in their outlook, making them hostile to some of the old folk customs.

Methodism had broad appeal and converted many of the poor at the bottom of society. Even so, Methodist converts in Wales tended to come from people who were in the middle ranks of Welsh society, such as farmers and craftsmen. These were people likely to be literate, sober, economically comfortable and willing to share their opinions. They were also inclined to be less deferential to the local squire, who was almost invariably in an alliance with the local Anglican priest.

The ordinary Anglicans found the Methodists lacking sufficient dignity because they were too passionate, too emotional, and much too enthusiastic. The Methodists found the Anglicans overly relaxed, smug, dry, ritualistic and mechanical. The Anglicans were hampered by the low level of funding for the Established Church which curtailed the provision of adequate services and teaching. After much dispute, a breach between Anglicanism and Methodism finally developed. The Methodists were expelled and set up their own rival Protestant denomination. Since they refused to conform to the Anglican ritual, they, along with other Protestant denominations, were called Nonconformists.

Soon Baptists and Congregationalists, old Puritan denominations, took up the techniques of the Methodists with considerable success. They differed from the Methodists in that they tended to welcome radical politics. By contrast, Methodists concentrated on converting individual people from the pathways of sin one by one and regarded obedience to the powers that be as important. Regardless of their differences, all of the major Nonconformist denominations swept the countryside from the late 18th century to the very early 19th century. The traditional culture of Wales, tinged with pagan revelry, was largely destroyed by them, including many old fairs, feasts and plays. The Nonconformists thoroughly prepared Wales for the serious, sober years of the earnest Victorians of the 19th century.

Education advanced hand-in-hand with the surge of Nonconformity. Griffith Jones, a Welsh clergyman, set up a number of circulating schools. Itinerant ministers went from parish to parish to teach. There were also evening classes so that servants and laborers could attend. It is estimated that the circulation schools taught more than half of the population of Wales to read by the 1760's. The Sunday school in the 18th century for both children and adults went beyond religious topics. Adults and children received instruction in the basics of reading, writing and arithmetic.

Charitable organizations also participated in furthering education in Wales. The Society for Promoting

Christian Knowledge taught poor Welsh children the basics in dozens of charity schools. Older children received vocational education. To staff their schools, the society hired churchmen who were grateful for an opportunity to supplement what were usually meager livings. There was also a Welsh Trust, a charitable organization to promote education which was noted for raising money among the Welsh living in London. Since much of this educational effort was carried out in the native Welsh language, the growing reading public stimulated the publication of books and other material in Welsh in the 18th century.

Education for the people at the lower end of society coincided with a growing interest in Welsh culture among the well educated. The study of old Welsh literature was fostered by several societies, supported in part from Welshmen who were doing very well in London. Antiquarians, many of them not Welsh themselves, became interested in ancient Welsh life and literature. They came to stress the identity of the Welsh as the direct descendants of the ancient Britons. At Oxford, antiquarians became interested in the origins of the Welsh language. There were also attempts to revive the craft of the Welsh bards and the ancient cultural gathering, the Eisteddfod, which had fallen into abeyance since the 16th century. In all of these efforts, fact, fiction and whimsy, as well as outright exaggeration and invention were swept together in the Welsh cultural revival. Modern scholars would face the task of sorting out this material.

Wales benefited from the Romantic Movement which swept western Europe in the late 18th century. The movement was noted for excitement over ancient and exotic subjects as well as wild, untamed nature. All of these impulses raised appreciation of places such as Wales because of its mountains, cliffs, waterfalls and ruins.

Before the 18th century mountainous areas were avoided by travelers because they were deemed stark, dangerous and forbidding. With romanticism they became thrilling and beautiful and have remained so in the popular imagination ever since. An English gentleman who traveled in Wales at this time wrote to his compatriots that Wales was "a strange country with wild scenery, rustic inhabitants and a strange language." He was among the first visitors to seek out romantic Wales, the fount of an endless stream of tourists which continues on to the present day.

While religious, educational and antiquarian developments in 18th century Wales were profound, nothing of particular consequence developed in politics. The Welsh gentry continued to dominate public affairs, arranging among themselves who would sit in the Welsh seats of the British Parliament. Most candidates were pre-arranged and took their seats uncontested. Very often, important gentry families passed on the right to sit for a certain constituency the way they passed on their estates. Wales had only 27 Members out the 558 elected from all over Britain after the union with Scotland.

When the leading gentry families fell out among themselves there were some electoral contests, but the differences were personal rather than ideological between candidates. When this did happen, respective landowners could count on the small number of electors to back their candidacy in their locality. Voting was out in the open.

A romantic painting showing the last of the Welsh bards as English forces invade Wales. There was an untrue rumor that Edward I killed Welsh bards.

There was no secret ballot and local people did not want to offend the landowner who gave patronage to local businesses and employment to them, to say nothing of rent and legal services. Overall, only approximately 4 percent of the Welsh population voted, or around 25,000 electors throughout Wales. Politics was definitely a gentleman's sport in the 18th century.

These gentlemen continued to become ever more anglicized, many of them marrying into English families. Their mansions and gardens took on an increasing English appearance. They spoke less and less Welsh, read English books, read some of the many English newspapers which now circulated in Wales, traveled to London and dressed and acted more and more like English gentlemen. They were, in effect, eager collaborators in anglicization.

Since Welsh gentlemen remained Tories, the Council of Wales, abolished in 1689, was not revived. The government in London, dominated by the other party, the Whigs, preferred to govern Wales directly rather than through a council which would be controlled by Welsh Tory squires. Their Tory sentiments did not extend to support the old Stuart line of kings, so when the Scots rebelled against the new, Hanoverian dynasty in the name of the old Stuart kings in 1715 and 1745, Wales did not participate. When the American Revolution burst upon the world stage, there was some support here and there for American patriots, but in general Wales remained Tory and docile. Only a few well-educated Welsh Nonconformists were inclined towards democracy at the time of the American and French Revolutions, a situation destined to change dramatically by the 19th century.

Llyn Peninsula in the north of Wales.
COURTESY OF THE WALES TOURIST BOARD.

One very minor event in Wales during the Napoleonic Wars did provide a dramatic moment in British history because it marked the last foreign invasion of the island. A few French ships landed a small force of unruly troops said to be convicts released from jail at Carreg Wastad in Pembrokeshire on February 22, 1797. This landing was only a minor diversionary effort to help a larger planned invasion of Ireland. French troops enjoyed a few days of looting but were then captured by the local yeomanry. On this occasion the Welsh swarmed forth patriotically to prevent the invasion of Britain by the hated French.

One story, perhaps apocryphal, that is, not founded on fact, emerged. Welsh women dressed in red shawls and black hats were seen approaching and were mistaken for soldiers by the French on shore. Jemima Nichols became a local heroine when she was supposed to have captured several French soldiers using only a pitchfork.

The French Revolution and Napoleon's rule called for radical destruction of the established hierarchies and churches throughout Europe and the granting of uniform freedom and justice for those below. Thrones and altars toppled as French armies triumphed. In Wales, only a few radicals espoused sympathy with the French Revolution, most notably Richard Price. Yet Welsh grievances were growing: Payment of tithes to the Established Church aggrieved Nonconformists; the legal system favored the wealthy; inflation, low wages and high prices for food spread discontent.

Welsh radicalism would not utilize this discontent and become powerful until the 19th century, after a large, politically conscious industrial working class came into existence and joined up with the increasing number of radical Nonconformists. As the 18th century drew to a close, the seeds of Welsh radicalism were sown and sprouting.

In the 18th century more and more English money came into Wales to lay the foundation for modern industry. English investments were put into copper works near Swansea; into iron and coal in South Wales; into scattered lead mines and into timber cutting. The Industrial Revolution had begun.

For most ordinary people, 80 percent to 90 percent of whom spoke Welsh as their everyday language, life went on

Footpath along the coast in Dylife.
COURTESY OF THE WALES TOURIST BOARD.

with its hardships in the 18th century. Many were bare-footed and preyed upon by lice and rats. Sanitary conditions were abominable, which meant that they stood a good chance of dying early from infections and disease. Work for most consisted of hard labor with hand tools for long hours. Those who had jobs in fishing, mining and processing minerals risked death or maiming at work from accidents. Habitations were dim and filled with smoky, fetid air. Unfortunately, countless romantics have overlooked these grim realities of pre-industrial Wales and have idealized an idyllic past.

Wales did retain a few romantic peculiarities as the 18th century drew to a close. The Welsh highlands had a few bands of brigands who lived by theft. In a few odd corners polygamy existed. Along the coast, ships were lured to crash on the rocks by mysterious false lights. Gangs of Welshmen could then loot the cargoes, claiming the right to salvage from wrecks, hence the name for this practice, "wrecking." All of these old practices would come to an end once the great force of the Industrial Revolution was let loose in Wales.

Wales and the Industrial Revolution — 1750 to 1850

The Industrial Revolution has been a worldwide phenomenon that has never ended because it is continually transforming parts of the globe with remarkable speed. The very first triumph of the Industrial Revolution was in Britain and during the process Wales was changed profoundly and permanently.

The world's first successful transformation of a traditional economy into an industrial economy occurred from the middle of the 18th century until the middle of the 19th century. It was actually a series of spontaneous revolutions and breakthroughs that simultaneously acted upon each other. An agricultural revolution utilized new crops and techniques, thereby raising food production and allowing more people to live in urban areas. A transportation revolution quickened the flow of goods and services and profits along improved roads, canals and, a few decades later, railroads. At the same time a revolution in technology put specialized, steam powered machines in operation that could produce with great speed and efficiency.

There was also an interacting demographic, or population, revolution that was as profound for England and Wales at that time as it is for other parts of the world today.

The British death rate fell dramatically in the late 18th century, a phenomenon whose complex causes are still a topic of debate among demographers. We do know that people married earlier, had more surviving children and were able to provide cheap labor for new industries as well as a mass consumer base for cheap, mass-produced goods. Before the Industrial Revolution, marriage in Britain was usually postponed for at least a decade after puberty, which came much later than it does today. This, along with early death from disease, had regularly limited the population. When masses of jobs opened up during the Industrial Revolution, earlier marriages took place with a consequent soaring birth rate. Although infant mortality remained alarmingly high, many of the large number of children born to most women lived on into reproductive age themselves and this is why the population totals pushed ahead. It was a phenomenon new to Britain in the 18th century and new to many places around the world in the 20th and 21st centuries.

When the economy "took off and became airborne," an economist's phrase signifying permanent, self-sustaining growth and development, major changes occurred swiftly and dramatically. In all previous history, most people lived in rural environments; in the new industrial society, the majority of people came to live in urban environments. In all previous history, people and goods traveled around at a top speed limited by the speed of horses; now rail transportation was ten times as fast. In all previous history, most craftsmen worked in small shops; after the Industrial Revolution, masses produced goods in great factories. Power throughout history had come from human muscle, animal muscle, water and wind; industrialization brought the steam engine. In the past, scarcity was the norm for most people; industrial production created a massive supply of goods whose cost per item dropped dramatically. Class structure changed also: urban environments needed more middle class and professional people, more lawyers, teachers, doctors, bankers and managers. Factories and mines demanded a huge number of workers to be concentrated in new towns. Rural people swarmed into these places to take the newly available jobs.

At the beginning of the Industrial Revolution, nearly all of Wales was agricultural, and most of the agricultural operations involved sheep grazing. Given the terrain and heavy rainfall, the agricultural revolution was not as successful in Wales as it was in England. Newly developed English improvements came to Welsh agriculture rather slowly and only where the lay of the land allowed. Nevertheless, food production decidedly increased as developments such as crop rotation and the production of new fodder crops got underway. In the past many animals were slaughtered in the fall because there was little to feed them in the winter. Greater numbers of animals were now able to survive over winter and continue to produce natural fertilizer.

Part of the agricultural revolution involved "enclosures," which meant that landlords put fences or hedges around formerly open land that had been used in common by local people for grazing and foraging. Enclosure eliminated the margin of survival for many Welsh families who consequently had to leave their farms. Several exceptionally wet years with poor harvests contributed to squeezing them out. Meanwhile landlords, stimulated by high prices for grain crops, raised rents on their tenants whenever possible.

Welsh estates tended to become larger as the agricultural revolution continued. Conflicts grew between the Welsh speaking, often impoverished and increasingly Nonconformist peasantry, and the anglicized and Anglican gentry. Some confrontations were so sharp that they became riots. Until the Industrial Revolution was well under way, agriculture still provided the main employment for most Welsh people. Yet conditions were so bad for Welsh agricultural workers that they were compared to the miserable Irish peasantry.

Wales was saved from the terrible fate of Ireland, a massive famine of the mid-19th century, by the fact that huge coalfields and substantial iron ore was available for industry. Rapidly expanding Welsh coal mines and quarries provided jobs for the teeming surplus population from the countryside. The population of Wales felt the same pressure of growth as the English and Irish populations. It rose from approximately half a million in 1770 to over a million in 1851. By that time only a third of the Welsh population was dependent upon agriculture. In Wales, unlike Ireland, there was an alternative to starving in the countryside for the surplus rural population.

During the time that Britain experienced the world's first great surge towards an industrialized society, Wales played its own important part in the process. Coal was the source of power for the steam engines that powered the factories, railroads and ships of the new Industrial Revolution. Wales contributed disproportionately in supplying coal, not only for domestic consumption but also as a

An early iron works during the Napoleonic Wars.

major British export. New techniques allowed deeper mining to exploit rich seams of high quality coal far below the surface.

Industrial production concentrated near the coalfields. It takes several tons of coal to smelt a ton of various kinds of ore, so ore was shipped to the coalfields. Before the Industrial Revolution, Welsh industry was small scale, localized and often run on a part time or seasonal basis. After the Industrial Revolution, Welsh production became massive.

Iron production became a key industry in Wales, doubling in output just from 1815 to 1830. Wales had all the resources for the iron industry: iron ore, limestone and

timber to make charcoal for smelting and to build processing structures. Later coke from coal replaced charcoal,
but timber was still needed for pit props in the coal mines.
It took four and a half tons of coal to yield a ton of iron,
so the iron ore was shipped in to iron mills located near
coalfields.

The capital and entrepreneurs needed to set the process
in motion came from England, mostly from the nearby city
of Bristol and from London. When the railway boom began
in the 1840's, the demand for rails made in Wales became
massive. Merthyr Tydfil, a hamlet in 1750, became a
leading center of the iron industry in south Wales, filled
with blast furnaces using coke. A new town of tall chimneys, Merthyr Tydfil in the early Industrial Revolution also
had sprawling slums, no public sewer, a riverbank covered
with rubbish and filthy streets.

Although Wales produced a large amount of bulk iron,
refinements were usually carried out in English cities,
Birmingham and Sheffield in particular. The same can be
said for several other industries that expanded in Wales
during this time. Britain's chief copper producing area was
in Wales, near Swansea. Tin was imported to Wales from
Cornwall for tin plating, a process that coated iron with
thin sheets of tin. Some lead mining and smelting was
expanded, yielding the by-products of zinc and silver. In
the northwest of Wales the slate industry played a role
similar to the coal industry in the south. Over 17,000 came
to work in the slate mines and some towns in the region
are dwarfed by the slag heaps that they produced. In
the northeast of Wales, industry was associated with the
famous operations in the Lancashire cities of Liverpool and

Manchester. Cotton textiles and pottery became notable industries in that part of Wales.

The transportation revolution affected Wales profoundly. Steam navigation increased shipping from Welsh ports, replacing overland trade with England to a considerable extent. The railroads produced remarkable and permanent changes in a very short period of time. Before the railroads it had taken days to travel to London. By 1850 it was a matter of hours. Before the railroads, few people traveled to Wales as tourists. Afterwards, Wales was visited by an ever-increasing tide of visitors from England and Europe seeking its romantic scenery. Even so, most of the

A romantic depiction of the great fiery furnaces of the Industrial Revolution.

123

main railway lines, the fast lines, went through Wales in order to link up England with Ireland via ports in Wales. Another aspect of the coming of the railways was that Welsh farmers could now ship perishable produce, such as milk, to populous English markets across the border.

Historical debates weighing the positive versus the negative effects of the Industrial Revolution have never ended, arguments that have been vigorously applied to conditions in Wales. Without doubt, the Industrial Revolution disfigured the Welsh countryside with its furnaces, chimneys, ugly installations, and rows of slapped-up houses. Towns sprawled without planning or control. As water supplies became polluted, diseases such as typhus, typhoid fever and cholera broke out frequently. Mortality rates in new industrial towns, particularly infant mortality, were very high.

Conditions for Welsh workers were often abysmal. Early quarries, factories and mines were extremely dangerous places and workers had to labor in them for excessive hours whenever there was work. Economic downturns were as frequent as booms, so workers could count on periodic short-term unemployment or sudden reductions in wages. Very often they had to pay their employers rent for their company housing and buy their groceries in company stores, called "truck shops," where prices were usually much higher than in ordinary shops. The people who first endured these conditions were almost invariably former country folk, likely to become disoriented in their new environment of bells, whistles, clocks and dangerous machinery.

An artist's rendition of a Welsh ironworks in the 1780's, showing the ugliness of industrialization.

There was an upside to early industrialism. A crowded Welsh-speaking society emerged in these new industrial towns, one that had its own Welsh cheerfulness and spirit. No matter how small and shabby their homes might be, there was plenty of cheap coal to keep them free from cold and damp. Welsh workers took pride in their workmanship as they handled the new processes. Above all, the industrial areas, despite all of their ugliness and harsh conditions, were a positive alternative to the lot of the miserable Welsh agricultural workers who earned only a third of what an industrial worker earned at the time.

Thanks to the new industrial towns, an appreciation of Welsh culture shifted from the scholars and antiquarians to ordinary Welsh people. Increasingly, the growing numbers of urban workers and the expanding urban middle class took up Welsh concerns, in particular the preservation of the language, the spread of Nonconformity, and popular opposition to economic oppression.

As Welsh people flocked into the new mining areas of southern Wales, Nonconformist chapels sprung up to minister to new communities and bind the newcomers together. The Established Church's parishes were usually centered far from the thriving new neighborhoods. In the chapels of the new mining communities, ordinary people learned how to debate and take part in administration. They also broadened their education and maintained their Welsh identity through their close connection with the chapel. One of the most striking examples was the development of mass choral singing in the new towns. To this day, Wales is celebrated for this artistic phenomenon.

The Welsh culture during the era of the Industrial Revolution was colored by class conflict and a drive for democracy. Workers were at a considerable disadvantage facing their employers, who would dismiss them for the slightest infractions, let alone opposition. Employers, who were often relatively new English immigrants to Wales, could count on the staggering population explosion to guarantee that any dismissed workers could be rapidly replaced. To make matters worse, the employers were likely to sit on benches as magistrates when conflicts became physical confrontations.

Many outbreaks of violence did occur. From 1839 to 1844, civil unrest and disobedience in the countryside took the form of the Rebecca Riots. Welsh men disguised in women's clothing attacked tollgates on roads and destroyed workhouses where the poor were forced to live in miserable conditions. High tolls on new roads were a major grievance in the early Industrial Revolution. Eventually the government reduced the tolls and amalgamated the toll roads more reasonably. Some unpopular landlords were also attacked as part of the hundreds of outbursts of violence in Wales. In Merthyr Tydfil, a very serious riot broke out in 1831 that eventually claimed at least twenty lives. Townsfolk burned down a building holding records of debts that they owed.

Organizing early unions was fraught with violence on both sides. Employers sought to break up unions by any means, and workers sometimes attacked non-union men and even employers. A secret group of workers called the "Scotch Cattle" was notorious for inflicting intimidation on non-union workers.

Robert Owen (1771–1858) was a famous Welshman closely involved with trying to build a union not just for Wales but for the whole British nation. Robert Owen actually became a very successful, kind and prosperous factory owner in Scotland before turning to radical causes, which included a type of utopian socialism. His national union failed, as well as his more diverse utopian schemes, but he is fondly remembered as someone who understood the psychology of workers and fostered the improvement of their lives.

The drive for democratic representation of ordinary people in the government took the form of a national movement throughout Britain called Chartism. The "People's Charter" called for such things as universal manhood suffrage, equal electoral districts, payment of Members of Parliament and the secret ballot. Chartism had strong appeal in Wales, where workers flocked to its meetings. Chartists were divided over the matter of tactics. Some favored education and peaceful demonstrations while others favored physical force to bring about what they perceived as needed change.

The Chartist experience for Wales has enduring fame because it led to the last rising against the government in British history. Wales was the only place where Chartism became so overtly revolutionary. In November of 1839, a large demonstration was planned for Newport. The more militant Chartists were rumored to want to seize the town as part of a radical national uprising for democracy. A former mayor of Newport, John Frost, a draper, was ambiguously implicated in these proceedings. Fighting broke out between several thousand Chartists and the local yeomanry. Before it was all over, ten men were killed in front of the Westgate Hotel. The hotel still stands and it may still be possible to see some of the damage from musket balls on its pillars.

Chartism faded by the late 1840's. By that time industrialism had permanently transformed Wales and given the province a new reputation. Henceforth Wales was regarded by conservatives as a potentially unstable area, rife with radical Nonconformists and radical workers who were wedded to a strange old culture proudly maintained by its ordinary people.

Chartist Rising in Newport.

Fighting among Chartists themselves. A major issue with them was whether they should use physical force or moral force in their campaigns.

The Industrial Revolution linked England and Wales more closely through industry, commerce, new roads and new railroads. A new division in Wales grew between that areas that were industrialized and those that remained agrarian, something of a parallel to the old Medieval division between *Wallia pura* and the marcher lordships. Anglicization was a strong force in the areas where mines and factories sprawled. Except for its upper, landed class, pre-industrial Wales had been readily inaccessible, isolated by geography, language and culture up until the late 18th century.

The dramatic increase in new jobs in Wales from the Industrial Revolution acted as a magnet to bring in English, Scottish and Irish workers. Wales was unusual among the areas of Europe because it had a net immigration rate in the 19th century despite a considerable emigration of Welsh people overseas. A large number of nominally Anglican English settled in south Wales and in the industrial areas adjacent to the English border. Masses of refugees from starvation in Ireland settled in Merthyr Tydfil, Swansea and Cardiff, and soon thereafter large Roman Catholic Churches were erected.

The English, Scots, and the Irish who settled in Wales were an important and growing segment of the population that could not be assimilated into Welsh culture. For them, Welsh culture and the Welsh language were increasingly associated with backward, rural areas. Increasingly, Welsh culture became least important in the areas of greatest new economic power. For many ambitious middle-class Welsh and their children, using the English language became absolutely necessary to get new and better occupations. Many Welsh came to live bilingual lives, reserving Welsh for home and chapel and English for education and work.

Thanks to the influx of outsiders during the Industrial Revolution, by 1871 over a third of the population living in Wales could speak only English, and their numbers were steadily growing. By 1901 only half the population could speak Welsh and only around 15 percent were monoglot Welsh speakers, meaning that they could speak no other language but Welsh. The Industrial Revolution had created a new and lasting division in Wales.

Subsequent centuries would see valiant struggles to revive Welsh culture and language in the face of overwhelming economic and social pressure from Wales' much larger and much more powerful neighbor.

Wales in the Victorian Era — 1837 to 1901

During the celebrated Victorian era, (1837–1901), Britain rose to become the foremost power in the world, dominant on the oceans, the possessor of the largest empire in history, and the world's leader in commerce, science, industry and prosperity. Possible rivals were preoccupied with internal affairs: The United States struggled with sectionalism and slavery while Germany was still divided into a large collection of German speaking states. Britain had never been so dominant and influential before the Victorian era and would never be as dominant and influential after it.

Wales shared in this triumph. Welsh mines and industries poured coal and metals into Britain's great world trade. Welsh soldiers fought valiantly in British uniforms to extend the empire worldwide. For example, the South Wales Borderers heroically defended Rorke's Drift in southern Africa against overwhelming numbers of Zulus. This exploit was celebrated, by the way, in the film *Zulu.*

The main political theme in Wales in the Victorian era was the linking of the Liberal Party with the causes of Nonconformity and Welsh nationalism. In Wales the Liberal party swept the old political leaders, the Anglican gentry, aside as reform bills dramatically expanded the British electorate downwards. The Reform Bill of 1867 increased the number of Welsh voters several-fold and the Reform Act of 1884 tripled it by extending the right to vote to farm laborers, miners and workers in the metal trades. Once the secret ballot was passed into law in 1872, the democratic thrust of Welsh politics was undeniable. Landlords and employers would no longer know how their tenants or employees voted and therefore could not exert economic pressure on them.

The Liberal Party was dominant in Wales from 1868 until after the end of World War I. Usually only around a third of the votes cast in Wales during this period went to the Conservatives, and a large number of these votes came from the areas close to the English border. By 1885, thirty of thirty-four seats in the British Parliament from Wales were occupied by Liberals, many of them practicing Nonconformists. Before World War I, almost every Welsh seat was held by a member of the Liberal Party. In 1906 the Conservatives did not hold a single seat in Wales.

In the Victorian era the Liberal Party stood for free trade, equal freedom for individuals, social equality and the end of various privileges enjoyed by the Anglican establishment. The Liberals fostered a stream of legislation to demolish the old bastions of hereditary privilege and discrimination. Their Conservative rivals were also reformers to an extent, since both parties sought to accommodate the ancient laws and institutions of Britain to the new, industrialized society. What came to make the progressive Conservatives distinct was their emphasis upon expanding the empire and the celebration of unified British nationalism.

A romantic painting of the defense of Rorke's Drift in the Zulu Wars. A Welsh regiment held the position.

Liberalism fit well with the professed virtues of the Victorian middle class, who saw themselves as moral, pious and committed to the work ethic. They sought to practice thrift, discipline, honesty, temperance, hard work, earnestness, cleanliness and obedience to God's Word. These virtues were, of course, the same preached in Welsh Nonconformist chapels.

Welsh Nonconformists increased their political activism in the 19th century. Early in the century they put themselves behind movements to campaign for an extension of the franchise and various Parliamentary reforms. Their denominational press in Welsh increased political consciousness and their congregations had long given Welsh people experience in participatory democracy. Another factor was simply that there were more of them in the 19th century as the Industrial Revolution generated more urban areas containing the new industrial working class and increasing numbers of middle-class tradesmen and shopkeepers. A religious census taken in 1851 showed that over 80 percent of the worshippers in Wales were Nonconformists of one denomination or another.

The Nonconformists had a burning political issue in this era: the continued existence of Anglican privileges in a Welsh society made up of a solid Nonconformist majority. Specifically, Welsh Nonconformists called for the disestablishment of the Anglican Church in Wales. This meant that the Anglican Church was no longer to collect tithes in Wales and that its endowment of land and other property was to be distributed to Welsh institutions. The Nonconformists wanted to finance a Welsh university, a Welsh library and Welsh county councils that would be in charge of local welfare and education.

In the past, the Established Church of Wales was noted for devoting itself to the spiritual needs of the largely English-speaking landowning families. Many of its bishops were occupied in other duties rather than tending their sees in Wales. This absenteeism decreased in the 19th century, as the Established Church sought to revive itself, but by the time most reforms were instituted, most of the Welsh wanted to see the end of its financial and official privileges.

Liberals took up the cause to disestablish the Anglican Church in Wales and the Conservatives bitterly opposed it, and in the process they generated what is said to be the longest word in the English language — "antidisestablish-mentarianism!"

Welsh Liberals were encouraged by the disestablishment of the Anglican Church in Ireland in 1869. They had the support of fellow Nonconformists in England who formed the Liberation Society. More pressure was put upon Parliament when riots broke out in Wales against the collection of the tithe. A disestablishment bill for Wales did become law in 1914 but it was suspended during World War I. It finally was implemented in 1920. As a result, the disestablished Anglican Church in Wales was renamed The Church in Wales. It remained spiritually linked to similar churches in Britain and the Empire and to the Episcopal Church in the United States. The Church in Wales gained an Archbishop at St. Asaph, meaning that the historic jurisdiction of the Archbishop of Canterbury over Wales' remaining Anglicans came to an end.

Disestablishment was not the only special cause of the Nonconformist Welsh Liberals. In 1881 the Welsh Sunday Closing Act was passed, which has been cited as the very first piece of modern legislation to recognize Wales as a distinct entity within the British nation. By this act Wales was treated differently than the rest of Britain in recognition of the fact that it was an area with a Nonconformist majority. What it did was close pubs on the Sabbath. Nonconformists tended to be strong teetotalers who were concerned about drunkenness, especially on Sundays.

Education was another keen concern of the Nonconformists throughout Britain. While newly-unified Germany went ahead to become the first nation to provide universal compulsory education, Britain lagged behind, locked in conflict between Anglican schools and Nonconformist schools. Two systems existed, the National Schools, which had Anglican support, and the British Schools, which had Nonconformist support. When the Conservative government provided finances for Anglican Church schools from local taxes in 1902, the so-called "Welsh Revolt" occurred. Welsh taxpayers simply refused to comply. Eventually universal education was provided throughout Britain with subsidies to existing church schools of whatever denomination.

The Local Government Act of 1888 established elected county councils to replace traditional forms of local government which the local gentry had long dominated in Wales through their positions as local magistrates. This act opened the door to democratic control of local government in Wales.

The greatest politician of the Victorian era was William Gladstone, who led the Liberal Party for decades. He was very sympathetic to Welsh, Irish and Scottish causes, and solid Liberal voting patterns from these outlying parts of the British Isles helped to keep him in office. Wales, Scotland and Ireland came to comprise what was called the loyal "Celtic fringe" of the Liberal Party.

Gladstone himself had an estate in Wales at Hawarden in Flintshire and lived there from 1839 to 1898. Also, his wife was Welsh. Gladstone started his career as a Tory, but as he developed he became more and more liberal. At the end of his career he was committed to democracy and noted for his kind, inclusive speeches in which he never spoke down to the electorate. At the age of eighty-two he was still calling for "justice for Wales." He was a

William Gladstone, the great Liberal leader of the "Celtic Fringe" of Scotland, Ireland and Wales.

committed, serious, sober Christian who spent much of his time in prayer. All of this endeared him and his party to the Welsh Nonconformists. It was said that half of the farmhouses in Wales displayed a picture of Gladstone.

The great failure in Gladstone's career, one that eventually split the dominant Liberal Party, was the inability to pass a Home Rule Bill for Ireland. Home Rule meant that the Irish would have their own Parliament and handle their own affairs while still remaining within the British Empire and dependent upon Britain for defense and trade—similar to the dominion status that Canada already enjoyed. Conservative English landlords, officials and voters wanted to keep Ireland joined to Britain as closely as Wales and Scotland were attached.

The Irish Home Rule struggle did raise the question of whether or not the Welsh desired a similar arrangement for their national existence. The actual devolution of Wales in the 21st century is, after all, a form of Home Rule. In the 1880s there were some efforts to launch a Welsh Home Rule movement, but antagonism between the more Anglicized south and the less Anglicized north caused it to flounder. Another movement surfaced from 1910 to 1914, but it also failed to make much of an impact. Most Welsh nationalists in the Victorian era strove for equality and recognition within the British system of government rather than Welsh separatism and exclusion from British life. The 19th century contrast between Wales and Ireland is striking in this regard. Irish Members of Parliament sitting at Westminster were solid nationalists demanding Home Rule; Welsh Members did not insist upon Welsh Home Rule.

A lack of enthusiasm for Home Rule did not mean that Welsh culture had faded in the Victorian era. On the contrary, there were many manifestations of a cultural renaissance that was chiefly literary and educational rather than political. A vigorous Welsh language periodical press had developed in the early 19th century and writing and publishing in Welsh had a new surge in the 1880's.

A major step forward for Welsh culture occurred when of the University College of Wales at Aberystwyth was opened in 1872. For a time it depended upon voluntary contributions from Nonconformist congregations. Colleges in Cardiff and Bangor followed in the 1880's, and Swansea would be added in 1920. These institutions became part of the National University of Wales, which was founded in 1893. All of these institutions stimulated an interest in Welsh history and literature, although the study of the Welsh language was not a key priority at first. Welsh was treated more as an academic subject rather than what it later became, the vehicle of national consciousness. English remained the dominant language in educational circles.

Part of the Romantic revival of the Victorian era celebrated old Welsh tales and revived the traditional literary and musical festival called the Eisteddfod. This festival became a regular feature of Welsh cultural life, something of an annual Olympic competition for poets and musicians in the Welsh language. Meanwhile ordinary Welsh people living in new industrial areas were able to enjoy a variety of cultural opportunities, ranging from singing festivals, theater societies, operatic societies, sporting competitions and activities centered around Nonconformist chapels. In addition, people could freely socialize in a variety of pubs and clubs. All of these social opportunities created a strong sense of belonging and support for individuals and families because they felt that they were enmeshed in a stable community and society.

One new social institution that developed for the Welsh working class in the late 19th century was the union. Indeed, for many Welsh workers the trade union lodge came to displace the chapel as the main gathering place for the community. Unions were established as a means to cope with economic pressures in the mines and factories. In the early 19th century, British trade unions were almost exclusively for highly skilled and regularly employed craftsmen, but towards the end of the 19th century, unions were extended to cover unskilled and semi-skilled workers and workers in such mass operations as mining. Although mine and quarry owners fought hard against the unions, organizers made considerable headway towards the end of the 19th century and in the early 20th century, at the time that industrial prosperity in Wales began to falter. One outstanding organization to emerge from unionization was the militant South Wales Miners' Federation.

Agricultural workers were worse off in this period. A great agricultural depression settled over all of Britain from the 1870's onward. The main cause was the availability of cheap grain and meat imported from overseas. When the vast plains of North and South America were opened to grain production in the 19th century, the new transportation infrastructure of railroads and steamships could get a bushel of grain to sell in a London market at a much cheaper price than a bushel of grain from Wales. Once refrigerated steamships were developed, Australian and Argentinean beef and mutton could sell in London at a cheaper price than beef and mutton shipped in from Wales. Meanwhile dairy farmers near the English border were in a uniquely profitable position because they could take advantage of the market for milk in expanding English urban areas nearby.

Rural areas in north and mid-Wales sank in depression. There was no relief from the old industries in these areas, copper mining, lead mining and woolen manufacturing, because these industries had decayed. Most Welsh

An Ulster poster against Home Rule for Ireland that depicts "Taffy" the Welshman in stereotypical garb.

tenant farmers continued to carry on their typically small operations of less than fifty acres with primitive techniques.

Landlords in Wales were also constrained by falling agricultural prices, which meant falling rents. They continued to be divided from their tenants by language, religion and politics. Landlords tended to be English speaking, Anglican and Conservative. Most poor Welsh tenants spoke Welsh, and tended to be Nonconformists who voted Liberal.

Due to the agricultural depression, similar hard times were experienced in Ireland, where the tenants were likely to be Roman Catholic, Irish-speaking and Liberal while the landlords were largely English monoglots, Anglican and Conservative. The big difference between Wales and Ireland was that the Irish took violent steps against their landlords, going so far as to kill some of them. The Welsh were much more passive, although they did agitate against high rents and the tithe.

Wales' Emigrants and Immigrants through the Centuries

The 19th century marked the simultaneous high tide of English immigration into Wales and the high tide of Welsh emigration to England and overseas. But immigration and emigration had been going on for centuries before and would continue to go on until the present day. This chapter will take stock of the dilution of the Welsh in Wales and the spread of the Welsh over the world from past to present.

The Irish had come to Wales from ancient times to the present day but the largest flow of Irish people to Wales occurred in the early 19th century. At first the Irish came as raiders from the sea and then as missionaries for Christianity. Since the Industrial Revolution in Britain coincided with the horrible years of famine in Ireland, great swarms of Irish workers arrived to help industrialize Wales by building the infrastructure of roads, railways and canals. Irish colonies settled in the Welsh industrial towns, where they offered to work for the very lowest wages. Welsh workers often resented the Irish for undercutting their wages and serving as strikebreakers.

Although the Irish and the Welsh were both Celts, speaking languages from the same Celtic family, there were noted differences between the two ethnicities. The Welsh were overwhelmingly Protestant and the Irish overwhelmingly Catholic. Temperamentally, the cultures differed also. The Irish tended to be adamant and out-spoken while the Welsh style was to be rather evasive in order to bring about conciliation.

Another group to arrive early in Ireland were Flemings from the Low Countries. They settled in one area of Wales and were noted for their loyalty to the English crown, which was manifested by their service as soldiers in the royal army. They learned English instead of Welsh in their new location.

Small numbers of Jews came to Wales in Roman times and thereafter, settling in modest numbers all over Wales. They were absorbed into Wales comparatively easily. Many became Christian converts. One Jewish industrialist, Alfred Mond, became a Liberal Member of Parliament from Swansea in 1910. When in the Cabinet, David Lloyd George, the most prominent politician from Wales, was sympathetic to the creation of a Jewish state in the Middle East.

Some gypsies came to Wales and gained a reputation as peddlers, horse dealers and musicians. Most settled down, married into Welsh families and eventually blended into the Welsh population.

The Normans, who invaded in the 11th century, brought more than their own French-Scandinavian stock. They imported soldiers from Brittany who could communicate with the Welsh in their Celtic Breton language. Trading and fishing connections between Wales and Brittany have continued to the present day.

Many Scots came to Wales in the 18th and 19th centuries, but in Wales, as in other parts of the British Empire, the Scots were noted for helping to manage English

Much of rural Wales remained rather backward in the 19th century. Here is a Welsh woman with her spinning wheel.

interests. They showed up as colliery agents and overseers or as gamekeepers on estates. When troops were brought into Wales for garrison duty or to preserve order, Scottish regiments were frequently selected.

In the 19th and 20th centuries, families of Spanish iron-workers and miners settled in south Wales. Some Italians also arrived, along with a relatively small number of other people from southern and eastern Europe.

In the post-war world, after the Second World War ended in 1945, the British Empire became a loose Commonwealth of independent states, and many immigrants came to England, Scotland and Wales from India, Pakistan, the West Indies, Africa and China, creating a substantial non-white minority in many towns and cities. Wales had long been the home of black seamen, and to a very considerable extent, they had been absorbed into the Welsh population. New immigrants soon comprised 1.5 percent of the population of Wales, roughly 42,000 people. They tended to settle in three places, Cardiff, where the minority figure was up to 4.8 percent; Newport; and Swansea. An increasing proportion are of mixed descent.

The Welsh see themselves as a tolerant, welcoming people, feeling that they share this spirit with the Danes and Swedes. The Welsh see their way of life as striving for understanding and harmony and displaying open-minded hospitality. They note the outbursts of racism towards minority immigrants in England and declare that "there is no problem" in Wales.

Nevertheless, even tolerant Wales had a few ugly incidents historically. There were anti-Irish outbursts in the 19th century and anti-Jewish and anti-Chinese riots in the early 20th century. In recent years the South Wales Police have reported some racially motivated incidents. Yet, these incidents are slight compared to the peaceful absorption of many groups in Wales over the centuries.

Of course, the newcomers and the Welsh can always join together to decry that great cuckoo bird in the Welsh nest, the English, the one ethnicity that has frequently exhausted Welsh tolerance because of its massive and often domineering intrusions and frequent disregard of the Welshness of Wales, an expression frequently used to encompass any and all manifestations of Welsh culture.

All during the times that people have been coming into Wales, Welsh people have been leaving. Welsh communities in London date back to the Middle Ages, and they continue in existence, constantly replenished by new people seeking fame, fortune or just regular, better paid employment in the metropolis. From the time of the Industrial Revolution a substantial Welsh community developed in Liverpool as well.

The most legendary of Welsh emigrants was a Welsh prince named Madog who supposedly sailed away with some Welshmen to discover America and settle in its interior in 1170! For a long time, rumors persisted about early explorers coming upon Welsh-speaking Indians. In 1792 a Welsh traveler named John Evans was sent out to America at the expense of a group of London Welshmen in order to find this lost tribe of Wales. He failed and did not live to see Wales again.

Even without Madog, the connection between Wales and America has been significant and enduring. Transatlantic passage was cheap by the 18th century, and many ordinary Welsh people settled in the colonies. Some founded Welsh speaking settlements in remote frontier areas and others lived in the new cities and attempted to publish Welsh-language newspapers and worship in Welsh-speaking chapels. Very soon many of the Welsh immigrants, especially the English speakers among them, assimilated and blended into the colonial population.

A surprising number of Americans have at least some Welsh ancestry. The easiest way to appreciate this fact is to contemplate the number of ordinary Welsh surnames that are common American surnames as well. They include Jones, Davies, Thomas, Hughes, Roberts, Evans, Griffiths, Lloyd, Vaughan, Powell, Hughes, Meredith, Williams, Rice and Price.

A large number of famous Americans have Welsh ancestry. Thomas Jefferson claimed that his father was born within sight of Mount Snowdon in Wales. The list includes (but goes far beyond) the following: Roger Williams, the founder of Rhode Island; Chief Justice John Marshall; Abraham Lincoln; Robert E. Lee; Jefferson Davis; James Monroe; Calvin Coolidge; Harriet Beecher Stowe, the novelist; D.W. Griffiths, the pioneer film maker; Frank Lloyd Wright, the architect; and Senator Hillary Clinton.

The Welsh were noted American patriots in the Revolutionary War era. Eighteen out of fifty-six signers of the Declaration of Independence were said to be of Welsh descent as were fourteen Revolutionary War generals. Patriotism continued in the Civil War era when the Welsh tended to support the North vigorously.

Welsh skills were in demand as the United States developed its industries. As the United States began to tap its extensive coal resources in the 19th century, large Welsh settlements were established near the coalfields in Scranton and Wilkes-Barre, Pennsylvania. The major coal mining area of Scranton boasted of the largest concentration of Welsh people outside of Britain. Welsh tinplate workers and iron miners were also employed at various sites in young, industrial America.

Overseas emigration from Wales went to many other parts of the world as well, particularly after the agricultural depression began in 1870. Canada, Australia, South Africa and Brazil all received Welsh immigrants. The most spectacular overseas venture was the creation of Wales' only colony overseas in Argentine Patagonia, or the southern region of Argentina. The colony was supposed to be entirely Welsh in language, culture and religion. Everyone over 18, men and women, were to have equal political rights. The first batch of settlers, 153 of them led by the Rev. Michael D. Jones, left for this relatively uninhabited area of difficult terrain in 1865. Their motivation was not unlike that of the Mormons trekking to Utah—both colonies were inspired by the Biblical search for a "Promised Land." The Argentine government was supposed to allow the Welsh colony to be autonomous, but meddling did occur over the years. Problems with indigenous people and the continuous encroachment of Spanish culture gradually eroded its Welshness, but there still is something of a Welsh presence in Patagonia today.

The Welsh appeared in smaller numbers in many distant places, including copper mines in Chile and iron mines in Spain. One Welshman, John Hughes, an expert on ironworks, was invited by tsarist Russia to develop iron and steel industries. One Russian town, Yuzovka, grew up around the foundries that once employed many Welsh immigrants.

Despite the departure of thousands of Welsh in all directions in the 19th century, their rate of emigration was considerably lower than that of English, Scottish or Irish immigrants overseas. In proportion to their respective populations, the English had four times as many emigrants; the Scots seven times and the Irish twenty-six times. It took the depression of the 20th century to force almost half a million Welsh into a mass exodus from their beautiful and friendly country.

Wales in the Early 20th Century — 1900 to 1918

The recognition of Wales as a separate entity gained several notable successes in the early 20th century and stimulated Welsh national consciousness. Royal charters founded additional Welsh institutions, namely a National Library at Aberystwyth and a National Museum at Cardiff. In 1907, a separate Welsh Department of the Board of Education was instituted to allow for some separate emphases for public schools in Wales. The House of Commons also established Standing Order 86 in 1907, which required that all Welsh Members of Parliament should be entitled to sit on committees to scrutinize legislation that dealt specifically with Wales.

Early in the Victorian era it seemed that prosperity in Wales would be guaranteed by the steam locomotive, steam ships and steam engines. All ran on coal and the best coal came from Wales and it was used worldwide. Half of the Welsh coal production was sold profitably overseas. Coal production doubled from 1870 to 1891 and almost doubled again by 1913. Eventually a quarter of a million men worked in Welsh mines, accounting for a large proportion of all British coal production. Huge docks were built at Cardiff, Swansea and Newport to ship coal to close and distant destinations. Cardiff became the chief of these ports and began to lay claim to being the new capital of

Wales, something that was finally confirmed officially in 1955.

Iron and steel production, tinplate production and slate quarrying all continued as important sectors of the Welsh economy in the Victorian and Edwardian eras. Nevertheless, some economic difficulties began to impinge upon profitability. Easily worked iron ore deposits were close to exhaustion and cheaper ore from other countries began to be shipped into Wales at a lower cost than ore mined in Wales.

While Wales still supplied 40 percent of Britain's coal exports in 1910, some new circumstances clouded the future of the greatest Welsh industry in history. The United States had become the largest producer of coal in the world and, closer to Wales, both Germany and Belgium began to exploit rich seams of coal. Welsh mining machinery was old and much less efficient than that of the new competitors for overseas markets.

Long dependence upon coal and iron made the Welsh economy vulnerable. Manufacturing, shipbuilding and engineering were underdeveloped in Wales. Other parts of Britain dominated these processes and offered greater diversity in employment opportunities. This lack of diversity had a devastating effect on the Welsh economy in the 20th century, when the coal industry languished and Welsh miners did not have alternate employment. The parts of Britain that had greater engineering and manufacturing experience began to take up the new chemical, electrical and automotive industries as they emerged in the early 20th century while Wales faced a future of staggering unemployment and idle mines.

Even when there was a high demand for Welsh coal, workers had serious grievances that fostered union membership. There were thousands of deaths from mining accidents during the Victorian and Edwardian eras. In just one incident in 1913 at Senghennydd, 439 men and boys were killed. Workers' wages were, for a time, tied to a sliding scale depending on coal prices. When prices were high, wages were high and vice-versa. Unions fought against the sliding scale and for higher wages. In the slate quarries, dust produced many cases of silicosis in quarrymen's lungs. Miners' homes continued to be poor and cramped, water supplies were often impure, and low wages guaranteed chronic malnourishment, a particularly unfortunate circumstance for children. All of these factors meant that life expectancy for men and women in mining communities remained in the forties.

Such conditions led to seething unrest in mines and quarries and confrontations between the new, militant unions and the mine owners in the form of strikes. The first wave of strikes was over recognition of the unions, and then for better working conditions and higher wages. Strikes occurred in waves from the 1870's to the eve of World War I in 1914. Sometimes the owners locked workers out of the mines and quarries. Sometimes workers sat down in the mines and forced the mines to remain idle. Sometimes soldiers were brought in to put down the striking workers and a few workers' deaths occurred.

The majority of Welsh people, whether they worked on the land or in the mines or were middle class townspeople, moved more to the left politically during the dawn of the 20th century. The broadened franchise, conditions in mining and the agricultural depression all contributed to this phenomenon. The Independent Labour Party, based on socialist principles, emerged and began to recruit members and voters in the mining towns. The South Wales constituency of Merthyr Tydfil was the first to send a Labour Party member to Parliament in 1900. He was a Scotsman, Keir Hardie, a robust democrat who showed up in the House of Commons dressed as a miner, complete with scarf and cloth cap, and to a flourish of trumpets!

For a time, the dominant Liberal Party cooperated with the fledgling Labour party, selecting only one candidate between them to stand against the Conservative candidate for a given constituency. For a time those few elected as Labour candidates were called "Lib-Labs." The era of Liberal control of the House of Commons would not be over until after the First World War. Until then, Liberal politics was energized by a group of young radical Liberals in their ranks. The foremost among them was the most famous Welshman of the 20th century, David Lloyd George, who was elected for Caernarfon in 1890 at age twenty-seven. He would hold that seat until 1945.

He was born in Liverpool of Welsh parents, but when his father died a short time after his birth he was sent off to be raised by his uncle, a shoemaker in Wales. Clever in school as in everything, he became a solicitor, or what Americans would call a lawyer. He was an ardent Welsh nationalist, meaning that he was always ready to criticize the aristocracy, landlords and royalty.

Lloyd George was a marvelously eloquent speaker and debater in Parliament and he used his talents to further the cause of Wales at every opportunity. He always

British soldiers going on an attack in World War I. Wales contributed a high percentage of its male population to the cause.

thought of himself as a Welshman first and foremost. The Welsh for the most part both appreciated and understood him, something that could not be said for many of his English opponents. When the minority nationality of South Africa, the Afrikaners, fought for independence against Britain in the Boer War of 1898–1901, David Lloyd George bravely took their side and incurred popular wrath in and outside of Parliament.

Lloyd George was much more than a champion of Wales in Parliament. He was an excellent negotiator, displaying great patience in difficult situations. He was highly intelligent and politically adroit. He could be at ease with all kinds of people. On the surface, he appeared to be open and emotional, with smiles and tears always impending. He had charisma mixed with the skills of a con man. He could win people over with an insider's conversation or a good laugh over something. On top of that he had a gift for showmanship. Slight in stature, he came to wear his hair long, like an old Welsh bard, and he grew a large moustache that made him look vaguely like an old Welsh warrior. To add to the effect, he liked to wear a big cape around his shoulders.

His talent, combined with his willingness to work long and hard, brought David Lloyd George to the front bench of the dominant Liberal Party in the early 20th century, where he came to be known as the "Welsh Wizard." In the government of Liberal Prime Minister Asquith he ascended to the second most important position, Chancellor of the Exchequer, in 1908. He wasted no time in preparing a radical budget for Parliament, the famous People's Budget of 1909. This budget sought to pay for new warships and social services at the same time by taxing the rich. The House of Lords refused to pass it and a constitutional crisis ensued, in which Lloyd George vigorously attacked the aristocracy in the name of democracy. What resulted was a constitutional shift in the form of the Parliament Act of 1911, which eliminated the veto power of the House of Lords over the House of Commons for all time. In his own way, the "Welsh Wizard" had helped to destroy the ancient power of the English aristocracy.

Freed from the legislative power of the Lords, the Liberal government proceeded to introduce a bill for the Home Rule of Ireland and bills that inaugurated the welfare state in Britain. Lloyd George was instrumental in bringing in schemes for health insurance and unemployment insurance, the cost to be paid for by employees, employers and by the government. These plans were modeled on the new and successful German welfare system. Later on in the century, another Welshman, Aneurin Bevan, would build upon Lloyd George's welfare legislation.

Lloyd George had a legion of associates in government but only one colleague who seemed close to him, the young Winston Churchill. At this stage of his life, Churchill, a scion of an English aristocratic family, was a Liberal. This friendship was remarkable, not just because of the striking class difference. Lloyd George's chief source of enduring fame was his leadership in World War I and for Churchill, his leadership in World War II.

World War I took a high proportion of young Welshmen into the military at the same time that it put the unemployed and underemployed and many women in Wales to work. A higher percentage of Welsh, per unit of population,

Lloyd George, the Minister of Munitions, inspects workers at one of the government factories.

enlisted than either the English, Scots or Irish. There were some anti-war protesters from left-wing groups and pacifist Nonconformists, but they comprised a very small minority. In all, 280,000 Welshmen joined up and 35,000 were killed. Among the dead was the famous Welsh poet, Wilfred Owen, who gave a voice to the mournful loss of life in that tragic, costly war. Robert Graves' *Goodbye to All That*, his famous autobiography, contains a long section detailing his service at the front with a Welsh unit.

For Britain and France, the losses in the war of 1914 to 1918 were roughly double those of World War II, even though World War II lasted longer (from 1939–1945) and World War I did not have heavy civilian losses from aerial bombardment. War memorials in small towns in Wales and throughout Britain show this conclusively: the list of dead for World War I is almost invariably approximately twice as long as the list of dead for World War II. There are no lists for the wounded, the fatherless, those who lost brothers or husbands or prospects for marriage. Wales shared fully with all the people of Britain in this great and horrible trauma of war.

In the early stages of the World War I, British forces in France found that they quickly ran out of ammunition for their heavy guns. The army faced a major crisis of an arms and munitions shortage. The government turned to the "Welsh Wizard" to conjure these supplies as fast as possible. Starting with a few chairs and secretaries, David Lloyd George built up a whole complex of government-owned factories employing an army of workers. As the head of the new Ministry of Munitions, he became known as "the man who could win the war." Initially, he had not been enthusiastic over the war, but when powerful Germany invaded little Belgium, a Welsh chord was struck in his consciousness and thereafter he was all for victory as soon as possible.

Impatience with losses led to impatience with the Liberal Prime Minister, Herbert Asquith, and schemes were mooted about to replace him with the Welsh dynamo who obviously could get results. Conservative and Labour leaders and dissident Liberals schemed behind Asquith's back. Just what role Lloyd George played in ousting his leader and becoming Prime Minister himself remains a murky mystery, but, given his quick deftness, it must have been considerable.

As a war leader, he successfully cut losses of shipping to enemy submarines by instituting the convoy system over the objections of senior naval personnel. He tried in vain to break the deadlock of slaughter on the Western Front but, finally, the Allies were able to wear down the Central Powers by attrition. He played a prominent part in shaping the Treaty of Versailles to settle European affairs after the war, but its flaws helped to bring on the next World War. He was more successful in arranging a peace treaty for Ireland in 1921.

Lloyd George's career as a member of the Cabinet came to an end abruptly when the Conservatives in his coalition government dumped him right after the war. Thereafter he was just a Member of Parliament, but a famous voice that was frequently raised on behalf of the poor and against the appeasement of foreign dictators.

Lloyd George is still appreciated and even revered in Wales today. In England he is much more of a controversial figure in history. His sexual escapades were notorious, even in an age when such matters were kept out of the media. In fact, he was known derisively as "the goat" because of his promiscuity. He also looted his campaign funds for his own personal benefit to the extent that he left office a rich man. He built up these campaign funds through flagrant business deals and the outright selling of government honors, distinctions and ranks through his control of royal patronage as Prime Minister.

A serious charge against him was that he cheapened and debased royal honors to the extent that the British aristocracy became diluted. One wit said that the Peerage had become the "Beerage" because so many rich brewers

David Lloyd George speaking to his Welsh constituents in 1919.

were given aristocratic ranks. To top it all off, one year before he died the man who warred upon the aristocracy and privilege all through his life became an earl! Incidentally, many Welsh people have been able to fathom a sweet irony in this. Regardless of whatever can be said of him, positively or negatively, David Lloyd George was undeniably the greatest Welshman of the 20th century.

Wales Between the Wars — 1918 to 1939

The costly victory of World War I was followed by a long and chronic depression, a grim, gray time for most Welsh people. Britain's depression was longer than the one in the United States, lasting from 1920 to the late 1930s. Wales was particularly hard hit because of the concentration of the Welsh labor force in coal and other depressed industries.

The government under Lloyd George had taken over the coalfields in World War I for the sake of smooth war production and after the war was over there was considerable pressure from the mining communities to continue nationalization. Nevertheless, the coalfields were returned to the owners in 1921. Unrest followed and veteran troops had to be deployed in south Wales to keep the peace.

Dependence upon the faltering post-war coal industry made Wales the most strike-prone region in Britain. Some of the strikes involved workers sitting in the mines for long periods in order to halt operations. In 1926 the great unions all over Britain confronted the establishment with a General Strike. Although this strike collapsed in a relatively short time, it led to a six-month stoppage of the coal industry in Wales. Afterwards wages were cut again, leading to chronic bitterness and despair on the part of the miners.

Wages were cut yet again in 1931 as coal prices fell. Unions protested furiously but unsuccessfully, calling for "not an hour on the day and not a penny off the pay." Nevertheless, by 1934 collieries employed half the men they employed in 1920. The whole coal industry was simply becoming less profitable. There was considerable competition from the exploitation of cheaper foreign coal that was easier to mine as well as competition from oil. Welsh seams of coal were old and tired and the equipment used in them was worn and outdated.

Unemployment for miners and other workers soared in the 1920s and 1930s. It stood at 13.4 million in 1925, went up to over 27 million in 1930 and peaked at 37 and a half million in 1932. Incidentally, some of the spirit of the coal mining communities can be gained from Richard Llewellyn's novel *How Green Was My Valley*, or from its old black and white film version. Llewellyn's novel is essentially a romantic story of idealized miners' struggle against the greed of the industrialists.

The British depression was mitigated by the development of some new industries, particularly the electrical, automotive, durable consumer goods and processed food industries. As war clouds built up over Europe in the late 1930s, industry turned to rearmament. Wales did not benefit as well as England from these new enterprises because of inadequate engineering skills, manufacturing plants and capital investment. The result was a mass exodus of unemployed Welsh to England, particularly to nearby Lancashire, the Midlands and to the southeast of England. Approximately half a million people, close to a fifth of the population, left Wales seeking jobs. Those who remained

Welsh workers emerge from a coal mine after a 20 week stay-in strike underground.

often lacked an adequate diet, wore old and patched clothes and lived in decaying housing.

These conditions led to a transformation of party politics in Wales. The Liberal Party faded from Wales as it faded in the rest of the nation, replaced by the more militant Labour Party. In fact, the coal mining areas of Wales became the greatest and most reliable stronghold of the Labour Party, with the possible exception of east London. Labour gained ten seats in Wales in the 1918 election and jumped up to twenty-five seats by 1929. Labour Members of Parliament elected from Wales in the interwar period were often trade union officials, miners or former miners.

In the depths of the depression some communists among the far left labor leaders were active in the coal mining areas, some calling for workers to arm themselves to resist the police. Nonetheless, the communists were not able to make many inroads upon the solid Labour Party support that continued to grow during the depression.

The Welsh nationalist party, Plaid Cymru, was founded in 1925 in the midst of the depression. Plaid Cymru campaigned for self-government for Wales. It had a slow start. There were only 500 members by 1930 and there was generally little interest in separatism or Home Rule for Wales or in a federal system. The party came to be associated with rural Wales and with those having literary interests. Plaid Cymru would have to wait over forty years before their appeal grew to the extent that they could elect their first Member of Parliament from Wales.

One of the founders of Plaid Cymru, its theoretician and sometimes president was a remarkable Welsh intellectual, Saunders Lewis (1893–1985). He is regarded as the architect of modern Welsh nationalism. He was a noted teacher, dramatist, poet and critic as well as a political leader.

He became notorious when he, a Baptist Minister and a schoolmaster, joined an unlikely trio of terrorists who burned down government buildings on a new British base for a bombing range. The construction of this installation required the destruction of an old Welsh landmark farmhouse. Lewis defended himself at a London court entirely in Welsh. He lost his university teaching job as a result and could not get another for many years, but he continued as the spokesman of a militant, new version of Welsh nationalism for almost half a century.

Wales During World War II and Its Aftermath — 1939 to 1951

Full employment returned in Wales during World War II. Wages and living standards rose to the extent that they outpaced wartime inflation. For the first time in a generation, there was a shortage of miners again as new munitions and other wartime factories competed for their labor.

Wales once again contributed more than its fair share of men and women in uniform. There was little opposition to conscription and general enthusiasm to fight the fascist menace in Europe. While Plaid Cymru, still a tiny nationalist party, declared its neutrality, most of its supporters were active in the wartime effort in some way. Only a few refused to serve.

Two Welsh cities were particularly hard hit by air attacks in the war, Swansea and Cardiff. The worst raid on Swansea, one of dozens, was in February, 1941, when 230 people were killed and the old town center and harbor were gutted. Cardiff also lost its city center and the oil tanks at Pembroke Dock burned for three weeks. A total of 985 civilians died from air raids in south Wales in 1941, which was the worst year for night raids. Throughout the whole war, thousands of Welsh people died or became homeless as a result of Nazi bombing.

The war brought new people to Wales. Thousands of women and children were temporarily resettled in rural

Wales to escape attacks on English cities. Later in the war, hundreds of thousands of German and Italian prisoners of war were sent to camps in Wales. British art treasures were also sent by the National Gallery to safe places in Wales.

In one of Churchill's more magnificent wartime speeches, he vowed that Nazi invaders would be fought on the beaches, in the towns and in the hills, but that Britain would never surrender. If the invasion had come and achieved some success, in all probability Wales would have played out its old, historic role once again by being the last stronghold to resist.

Churchill's premiership did not last quite as long as the war. He was ousted between the victory over Germany and the victory over Japan. To his surprise and the surprise of millions throughout the world, a Labour government came to power with a clear majority of seats in the House of Commons. They also took nearly every seat in Wales. This new government brought about profound changes throughout Britain. The government of Clement Attlee carried on the so-called "Quiet Revolution" of 1945 to 1951 that created the modern welfare state and the mixed economy of socialism and capitalism that have, to a considerable extent, continued in existence to the present day.

The war had made government planning respectable. State direction of resources and care for the victims of the war showed what government could do to improve conditions. Labour Party leaders were fully involved in the process because the wartime government was a coalition government of all parties.

The impact of the "Quiet Revolution" on Wales was profound. The war had left Wales with a trained industrial workforce. Since the government gained the power to allocate new factories to areas needing them under the Distribution of Industry Act of 1945, new, light industry came to Wales, deliberately placed in the more depressed areas. Nationalization of key economic sectors affected Wales even more than England. The coal industry, railroads, docks, gas, electricity, and the iron and steel industries all became public corporations. The private sector, meanwhile, was to be carefully regulated.

Unemployed Welsh miners waiting for slag from the coal mine to drop. The workers would then seek to glean pieces of coal from the slag.

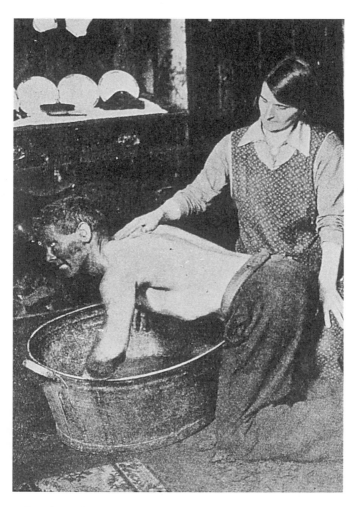

A South Wales miner's bath during the Interwar era.

Public sector social services were dramatically expanded. Everyone was to be assured of the basic necessities of life, food, housing, health care, clothing and education. The poor were no longer to be haunted by the specter of financial catastrophe from illness, old age or unemployment. The hard political decision to increase public spending while decreasing private spending through taxation was bravely taken. As a result of these quiet but dramatic changes, prosperity and security in Wales followed World War II, which was in sharp contrast to the aftermath of World War I. Unemployment levels remained low. Government subsidies and government jobs kept the economy buoyant.

The coal industry remained problematic, despite nationalization, which brought a flow of new investment for modern technology, including mechanized coal cutting, hydraulic pit props, and power loading. In 1947 the number employed in the coal industry was only 115,000, down from 270,000 in 1927. By the 1980s, the competition from oil, nuclear power and natural gas to serve energy needs caused many coal mines to close and prompted many miners' strikes. When unemployed in the post-war era, many miners became depressed and had problems with alcohol and family stability.

Wales endured one disaster from the coal industry when an unstable slagheap engulfed a school in Aberfan in 1966, killing 116 children and 128 adults. The tragedy became a major worldwide news story.

One profound change affecting everyone in Wales was the establishment of the welfare state. The historic origin of the welfare state was very strongly influenced by Welsh

A house threatened by a slag heap.

leadership. David Lloyd George's health and unemployment measures from the Liberal era before World War I
were augmented by those of James Griffiths, a key
member of the Attlee government. He began as a Welsh-
speaking miner. He rose through Labour ranks and was
able to usher in expanded benefits for all. Eventually, he
became the first Secretary of State for Wales.

Another Welshman, Aneurin Bevan (1897–1960), was
the most dramatic and striking of all the post-war Labour
ministers. It was he who inaugurated the National Health
Service, which remains, despite its many critics, the most
popular aspect of the welfare state. As the Minister of
Health, he patiently negotiated with doctors, dentists and

Aneurin Bevan, a great orator and left-wing politician from Wales. He was Minister of Health in the post-war Labour government.

hospital administrators to bring about nationalization as the capstone of the Labour government's achievements. Winston Churchill, a political opponent, sarcastically referred to him the "Minister of Disease."

Because of their similar names, Aneurin Bevan is sometimes confused with another Labour minister, Ernest Bevin, who was from Bristol, England. Bevan is best remembered as a powerful radical socialist orator who was close to expulsion from the party for being too far to the left. He was the sixth of ten children of a Welsh miner and he became a miner himself in 1911. He opposed World War I and became a Labour Member of Parliament in 1929. He opposed the appeasement policies of Neville Chamberlain harshly. After his work with health, he worked on slum clearance and public housing. His personality was stormy, a quality that was clearly reflected in his powerful speeches. Only Churchill was said to be a better speaker in the House of Commons at that time. "Bevanism" became an adjective to describe the far left of Labour. This group felt that the economic assistance given to Wales by the Attlee government was not enough. Eventually Bevan opposed the leadership of his own party.

Bevan differed from James Griffiths over devolution for Wales. Griffiths constantly sought to make Wales a distinct administrative unit and Bevan joined Prime Minister Atlee in believing that strong central planning would take care of any regional problems. Since Wales was increasingly benefiting from support by the national exchequer, Home Rule did not seem as a wise policy at that time to many Welsh Labourites.

The "Quiet Revolution" taxed the remaining large estates in Wales so heavily that most fell into decay or were taken over for tourists by the National Trust for historic places. Most Welsh farms continued to be small scale. Welsh agriculture was not very profitable in the post-war world despite new subsidies. Consequently, rural depopulation continued after 1945. Some economic infusions came from increasing tourism, from English people seeking a second home or from the elderly English and returning Welsh seeking a pleasant and relatively inexpensive place to retire.

The Long Postwar Road
to Devolution — 1951 to 2001

At the end of the Labour Party's "Quiet Revolution" it seemed that Wales was ever more connected to Britain. The Labour Party was dominant in Welsh politics and based in London; the welfare state was universal throughout Britain and Welsh workers belonged to British based unions. The English language was constantly making inroads on the dwindling areas of Welsh speakers, coming across on the radio, cinema and the new television industry. It even remained dominant at universities in Wales. For all these reasons, Welsh nationalism seemed destined to fade, as Wales became less Welsh and more British.

Just the opposite happened. Welsh nationalism revived powerfully and took various forms. Some Welsh nationalists strove for separate institutions and looked forward to devolution, which meant a federal arrangement allowing the Welsh to deal with their own affairs through their own assembly. Others took a much more militant path, using physical violence and obstructionism to force recognition of their demands. Some concentrated on preserving Welsh culture by keeping the language alive.

Modern nationalism has become a passion for several other peoples besides the Welsh who see themselves as a "submerged nationality." North Americans are familiar with the militant French-speakers of Quebec. The Basques and Catalans confound Spanish authorities and the Kurds disturb governments in Turkey and Iraq. For Welsh or other nationalists today, love of the nation and its culture can become a secular religion and a constant obsession. At worst, nationalism becomes an addiction, often as intolerant as racism; at best, it fosters pride, self-respect and historical perspective.

Modern civilization pushes humanity towards uniformity, so that most people tend to dress the same way, talk over the same topics and pursue the same interests and activities. Globalization has made the tendency towards homogeneity worldwide. A growing world market shapes a world civilization increasingly connected through computers, telephones and television. Huge government establishments and enormous, powerful multi-national corporations have become dominant.

Nationalists resist these forces by stressing the differences between their own particular group and the rest of the world. Often this sentiment is carried over into the "narcissism of petty differences," or the self-love of exaggerated petty differences. Nationalists have to contend against a world where consumer goods, fast foods and popular culture have become entrenched in the national homeland. Provincialism, regionalism, the small, the peculiar and the particular are dwarfed and endangered. When faced with such powerful global forces pushing towards uniformity, conformity, common interests and sameness, many particular groups in the world have gone to great lengths to stress their separateness, distinctness and unique cultures.

These global conditions certainly provide one of the main explanations for the recent resurgence of Welsh nationalism. Another important motivation has been a continuation of the old struggle to maintain a distinct Welshness against the seemingly overwhelming influence of its much larger and much more powerful neighbor.

The growth of Plaid Cymru reveals the surge of postwar nationalism. By the 1960's it became an attractive alternative for Welsh voters who were angered by both of the major parties. Although Plaid Cymru picked up only a very few seats in Parliamentary elections, it came in as an ever stronger second to many victorious Labour candidates as well as to the few Conservative candidates that were elected.

At first, Plaid Cymru support came from some teachers, writers, students and ministers who were regarded as romantics, or rural Welsh speakers who were seen as reactionaries. As time went on, more lawyers, union members and others cast their vote for the party. The Plaid Cymru platform was to win Home Rule for Wales rather than separation from England. Partnership and confederation with England, not separatism was the stated goal of the party.

A radical fringe of nationalists created the tiny Free Wales Army, which made a nuisance of itself by bombing water pipes bringing Welsh water to England, bombing English government offices and burning down empty vacation cottages bought by English people as well as attacking the real estate agencies that sold them. They were particularly active in the Conservative Thatcher era of the 1980s, but insignificant compared to the I.R.A. and Ulster Volunteers in either numbers or effect.

A view of Cardiganshire coast of Wales.

The event that brought the Free Wales Army into existence was the building of the Tryweryn reservoir by damming the Tryweryn River. The dam flooded a whole Welsh town and surrounding farming area, whose inhabitants had to be relocated. The purpose of the dam was to bring abundant Welsh water to the conurbation of Liverpool and Manchester. Since it was done arbitrarily by English bureaucrats without even consulting the Welsh, nationalists were outraged. The more extreme members struck back by trying to blow up a pylon carrying power to the site, dumping oil into the dam site and blocking access roads.

The Free Wales Army had many maudlin and ludicrous aspects. They did much swaggering, posturing and

Caernavorn Castle, where the princes of Wales are crowned.

drinking. Many schemes and plans never got beyond the pubs where they were hatched. While they boasted of having hundreds of thousands of members and heavy guns and even planes hidden in the mountains, they only had a few dozen members who regularly paid their dues. As might be expected, the media made much of their activities and filmed some of them playing soldier in the country wearing guerrilla military garb. By the time their bombing campaign ended, two people were dead, both nationalists who had mismanaged a bomb themselves. In addition, one child who had accidentally come upon a bomb was maimed.

A significant event for the militant nationalists was the investiture of Charles as Prince of Wales in 1966. Most

Welsh people looked forward to the event and did not want it marred by what they perceived as a group of fanatics and hooligans. Those who opposed the ceremony saw the investiture as the recognition of Wales as a quaint and colorful extension of England. There were also grumbles that the royal family made much of its vacations in Scotland and enjoyment of Scottish customs without comparable appreciation of Welsh culture, despite Charles' crash course in Welsh. Bomb threats guaranteed that security was tight during the ceremony. Eventually a handful of the Free Wales Army members were arrested and some were sentenced to less than two years in jail.

Many other minor acts of civil disobedience occurred to foster Welsh nationalism, most of them involving insistence upon the use of the Welsh language. English road signs were destroyed and Welsh graffiti was sprayed on many rocks and bridges. Protests demanded the use of Welsh for a variety of public purposes. Parents tried to register the births of their children in Welsh and were fined for not using English. Sit-ins occurred in post offices to demand bilingual forms. Some refused to pay their car registration taxes because the forms were only in English.

The British government and British firms made concessions. Banks voluntarily provided forms and checkbooks in Welsh, and the post office vans were inscribed in English and Welsh. The highway signs, birth and death registers and hundreds of official forms and documents commonly used were issued in both languages. Finally, a Welsh Language Act was passed by the British Parliament in 1967 sanctioning the special status of the language in official transactions. Welsh could then be used in courts and local government with the same status as English.

While all of this militancy was displayed by a relatively small number of Welsh people, serious steps towards the devolution of Wales were taking place at the highest levels. A Council for Wales was established in 1948, a Ministry for Welsh Affairs, or the Welsh Office, was created in 1951 and a Secretary of State for Wales was appointed in 1964. At first his powers were limited to Welsh housing, transport and regional economic planning. In the next decade the Secretary's Office took over health, education, industry, and agriculture as well. Moreover, this gave Wales an ombudsman in the Cabinet who could do such things as keeping Welsh rail lines from being shut down and valleys from being flooded.

The Labour Party debated offering the next step, which was a Welsh Assembly. The Conservatives were hostile to devolution and stood as "one nation Tories." Conservatives in the Thatcher era were noted for pushing centralization in the name of modernization, often at the expense of local government. Most of the Welsh were particularly unhappy when the Conservatives were in power because not only were they governed by a party that gained only a minority of votes in Wales, but the Conservatives appointed Englishmen to be Welsh Secretaries. Labour, meanwhile, had many Welsh leaders including Michael Foot, James Calaghan, and Neil Kinnock.

From 1974 to 1979, the Labour Party had been sharply divided over devolution. Those against devolution were worried that it would produce a cleavage between Welsh speakers and English speakers and tension between the

Modern Swansea harbor, substantially rebuilt after it was gutted by bombing in World War II.

northern and southern regions of Wales. Beyond that, devolution of power, however limited, might be a big step down a slippery slope that would lead eventually to separation. The counter-argument was obvious: Plaid Cymru was taking away Labour votes to the extent that it was taking some seats from Labour in Parliament. Proposing devolution would take the wind out of their sails by expropriating their main cause.

Finally, a Labour Party majority passed a pledge to establish a directly elected Welsh assembly providing that it would be approved in a referendum by Welsh voters in 1979. According to the proposal, the Assembly would have control over many of the functions of the Welsh Secretary, namely health, social services, education, development and local government. Yet it lacked powers to tax and the British Parliament was to retain a veto over its legislation.

Many felt that this bill did not go far enough while others felt that it went too far. The voters were surprisingly apathetic and negative. The devolution vote of 1979, voters were five to one against the scheme and less than half voted. Devolution in Wales was shelved for the time being.

Scotland, meanwhile, had a stronger turnout for its proposed devolution, which failed much more narrowly. The Scottish nationalist party was much stronger than its equivalent in Wales and a Scottish Secretary had existed since the end of the 19th century.

The promise of devolution for Scotland and Wales was one of the top priority campaign issues that brought the Labour Party to power in the election of 1997, a year that became a turning point in Welsh history. Running on a platform of devolution for both Wales and Scotland, Tony Blair's party won a stunning victory in Wales, leaving the Conservatives no seats at all in the principality. After this victory, the quest for devolution was announced in the Queen's speech in May, and the Secretary for Wales, Ron Davies, announced in July that Welsh voters would have a second referendum on the proposal of devolution. It took place on September 18, 1997 and passed, but only by the very thinnest of margins, what has been called a "wafer-thin" majority. Moreover, only 50.3 percent of the 2.2 million eligible voters in Wales turned out, and the measure passed by 50.3 percent to 49.7 percent, a mere .6 of one percent, or 7,000 votes.

In Scotland, devolution was passed by almost three quarters of the voters. Questions were raised in Wales about the legitimacy of the Assembly since it was acceded to only by a minority of those living in Wales. Nonetheless, devolution allowed the election of the first democratically elected assembly in Welsh history. Many regarded provincial democracy as a great step forward.

The Prime Minister, noting the narrow vote and seeking to lessen the fear of separation, said that the government needed to "convey the message that devolution is nothing to do with taking Wales out of the United Kingdom." Meanwhile, the Conservative opposition called upon the government to "think again" before going ahead with Welsh devolution.

Why was it so close and why did so many people stay home instead of voting? Much speculation has ensued. Certainly Welsh nationalists guaranteed a yes vote in the west. But the northeast and the heavily populated southeast voted no. These were the regions more heavily assimilated to England, with fewer Welsh speakers and more people who had moved from England. Indeed, many commute to England on a daily basis, or are attached to English commercial interests.

Many no voters feared growing separation from England, and argued that, unlike the Scots, the people of Wales did not have a unified culture and history. After all, they argued, England had ruled Wales for over 700 years and administered Wales directly for 600 years. The desire for statehood was not as strong as in Scotland, nor were Welsh institutions as developed as Scottish institutions were at the time when England asserted its control. After all, Scotland had a Parliament of its own from the middle ages to its dissolution in the early 18th century.

Scotland did indeed gain more autonomy when its devolution passed in a referendum held one week before the vote in Wales. Instead of an Assembly, Scotland regained its own Parliament again, which retained the right to raise or lower taxes. The Welsh had no such power, and some have argued that if devolution meant a more authoritative body in Wales, more people would have voted.

One argument against devolution cited the fact that Welsh representatives had sat in the British Parliament since the 15th century, where they voted on English and

One of the many bilingual signs found all over Wales.

Scottish matters, as well as on Welsh matters. Therefore, English and Scottish representatives were entitled to continue to vote on Welsh matters. The opposing view was that the Welsh representatives would always be a very small minority in the House of Commons. Another criticism of devolution was that it would create another layer of government and bureaucracy and thereby turn out to be yet another burden for the taxpayers.

The Welsh Assembly came into existence in Cardiff a year after the passage of the Government of Wales Act in 1998. Two-thirds of its members, forty out of sixty, were elected in the traditional winner-take-all manner of Parliamentary elections, but twenty were named on the basis of proportional representation. They were taken from lists drawn up by the respective parties. Therefore, if a party gained 50 percent of the popular vote, it would have the right to appoint ten more members. If a party gained only 10 percent of the vote, it would be able to appoint two members.

The net effect of proportional representation combined with traditional voting was that Wales now has a functioning four party system rather than Labour dominance. When the first Assembly gathered in 1999, proportional representation secured the Liberal Democrats three additional seats, Plaid Cymru eight additional seats and the Conservatives eight more also. Overall, Labour was disappointed that it closely missed having an absolute majority of the sixty seats.

The tasks put before the Assembly was to develop policy and implement decisions in: agriculture, ancient monuments and historic buildings, culture, economic development, education, the environment, health, highways, housing, industry, local government, social services, sport and leisure, tourism, town and country planning, transport roads and the Welsh language. The Secretary of State for Wales had been responsible for many of these matters in the immediate past. Powers over what are called home affairs, police and the judiciary in particular, are retained by the British government at Westminster as are powers over defense, foreign policy and fiscal matters, including taxation.

The Assembly's primary responsibility was to take charge and set priorities for a block grant of £7 billion (or $12 billion), which was the annual budget, formerly the responsibility of the Welsh Office of the national government. Meanwhile, the Welsh Office was to be considerably reduced in size. Similarly, a large number of quasi-autonomous organizations pertaining to Wales would be abolished. Scores of committees controlling local and regional matters in Wales now came under the management of the Assembly and its elected chief executive, known as the First Minister.

Devolution is easier for Americans to understand than it is for many British people. In essence, devolution set up something of a federal system, with Wales and Scotland gaining the powers of local representation and local control similar to those enjoyed in each of the fifty American States through their governors and legislatures.

The Economy of Contemporary Wales

When Labour brought Britain into the European Economic Community, Wales gained many economic opportunities. In most of the 20th century, the Welsh economy had not grown as quickly as the rest of the United Kingdom. Job creation had been a chronic problem. Recently, companies from Britain or the Common Market or Japan and the United States have improved the Welsh economy by locating important operations in Wales. For example, high tech jobs in computer related companies such as Sharp and Sony have provided many jobs in Wales. So has considerable government intervention via subsidies and government jobs.

Foreign-owned companies make Wales a net importer of investment and create some of the best jobs in manufacturing. The British government enables companies to establish themselves in Wales by providing generous incentives, the cost of which is borne by British taxpayers. Many foreign firms are concentrated in the electrical, electronic engineering, motor parts and chemical manufacturing sectors. Perhaps the greatest incentive for them to relocate in Wales is that they have access to labor that is cheaper than at home or in other parts of the European Union. Gone are the days when fully employed Welsh miners and steelworkers commanded handsome wages in what were key industries. Now the descendants of these highly paid miners and steel workers work in light industry, in offices with computers and in service jobs.

Manufacturing employs approximately 30 percent of men and 12 percent of women in modern Wales, but usually not in the best jobs, which are those of managers, scientists, engineers and technologists. Wales regularly supplies a high percentage of manual workers for firms whose headquarters and research operations are elsewhere. Assembly plants are common in Wales. Many businesses only have branch offices in Wales and, in hard times, branch offices are more likely to close or cut employment.

As in most mature modern economies, the service sector has grown enormously. In Wales it employs around 34 percent of men and 37 percent of women. New jobs have been created in banking, insurance and finance. Of course, a very large number of service jobs are in the public sector, particularly in health and education, to the extent that Wales leads the rest of the United Kingdom in the percentage of public sector income. Nevertheless, by their nature public sector jobs make relatively lower contributions to the gross domestic product than other jobs.

One of the major expanding service industries is tourism, spurred by the huge growth in tourism globally. Of course, English visitors from nearby cities have flocked to the Welsh coast for centuries and in recent decades their vacation trailers, called caravans, create many shabby, temporary communities in the summer months. Recently the influx of visitors from all over the globe has massively expanded the Welsh tourist industry. In terms of income, the tourist industry has become a genuine Welsh gold mine.

Romantic images are the stock and trade of the tourist industry, and Wales does lend itself well to such promotions. Prospective tourists are lured to a romantic land of gentle beauty, of historical legends, mysteries and fantasies, of poets and singers, castles, cottages, old small towns, flowing streams, sheep speckled hills, majestic mountains, flowers, songs, druids, ghosts, spirituality and gentle wildness. It is advertised as a veritable paradise for pony trekking, rock climbing and hiking.

In addition, there are heritage sites built on purpose for the tourist industry. These attractions go far beyond museums by becoming interpretive centers where a nationalistic Welsh sense of history is reinforced. Old coal mines and slate quarries now have a steady stream of tourists from all over the globe, most of them herded in groups while taking pictures or filming.

Wales is portrayed as a place where the indomitable Celtic spirit of local people lives on despite over seven centuries of domination and influence from their English neighbors. Wales is described as a small nation with a great heart, its people bound in an enduring Celtic fellowship.

Agriculture has continued to suffer adversities in the contemporary era despite the influx of substantial E. E. C. (European Economic Community) farming subsidies. Small farms continue to struggle and many of them fail. In fact, the rural heartland of beautiful and rugged mid-Wales has continued to suffer depopulation. Overall, agriculture only employs a minor portion of the workforce today. Most farm income comes from cattle, sheep and milk, but when the number of farmers is added to those working in fishing and forestry, the sum is less than 8 percent of those employed in Wales.

Rural Wales continues to occupy a special place in the imagination. In a typical rural environment, consisting of poor and marginal uplands, an integrated, cooperative, religious, family-based, democratic Welsh society has been long celebrated. But the impact of modern urban society, with all its English influences, has eroded traditional Welsh rural society considerably. The very unprofitableness of these farms, which demand long hours for low wages, has led to flight from them by young people. Concurrently, chapel membership and rural school enrollment has fallen. Meanwhile the number of houses occupied by the elderly, pensioners and retired people has risen. Poverty in rural Wales is underreported and scattered, but it may really affect a quarter of the households.

Most jobs in rural Wales are also now in the service sector, in retailing, tourism, education, health and welfare. Actually, most people in rural Wales now have only a tenuous connection to agriculture. Whenever industry has been deliberately relocated to rural Wales, it has brought an influx of English managers and executives enjoying a higher standard of living, including housing. Considerable "gentrification" has taken place and many old places have been refurbished. Other English people have bought second homes in rural Wales, often turning most buildings in some villages into absentee housing. All of this means that rural Wales has increasingly become the location of an English-speaking middle class that often disregards traditional Welsh culture and behaves in ways that are new to the region.

Worms Head on the Gower Peninsula.
COURTESY OF THE WALES TOURIST BOARD.

Welsh water resources have become increasingly important as urban England requires increasing amounts of water. Global warming and the very unusual recent appearance of droughts in England indicate the possibility of a more massive need for Welsh water in the future. It is estimated that Wales uses approximately 150 million gallons of water daily out of 950 million gallons available.

Physically Wales and England have become closer because of the extension of the M4 motorway from London to south Wales via the Severn Bridge, which was opened in 1966. Although many old, slow and quaint train services in Wales have been retired, powerful Intercity trains, capable of 125 M.P.H., have made trips between London and South Wales quick and easy.

One of the most dramatic changes in the economy of Wales from the World War II until the present has been the greater employment of women. In the 1970's, only a third of the workforce was female; now it is close to half, a proportion now matching the rest of the United Kingdom. Growth in the service sector and the decline of coal, iron and steel advanced the employment of women considerably. Women have taken a high proportion of the jobs in finance, insurance, tourism, leisure and the media.

Legislation helped bring about this change. A ban on married women in some jobs in the public sector was lifted early in the 1970s. Membership in the E. E. C. and the passage of a Sex Discrimination Act and an Equal Pay Act brought the whole United Kingdom in line with European-wide directives. The pay gap between men and women doing equal work was reduced from 26 percent in 1977 to 13 percent in 1997. As in the United States, fewer Welsh women than Welsh men have managed to get to senior posts so far.

Overall, the United Kingdom is one of the more affluent nations in the world, but Wales continues to be the poorest region of Britain, but poor only in relative terms. It is similar to saying that someone is the shortest of a group of very tall people.

Current economic problems include unemployment rates that remain higher in Wales than in the rest of the United Kingdom. Consequently, social security benefits make up a higher proportion of incomes in the principality than elsewhere in Britain. The gross domestic product per head remains lower in Wales than elsewhere in the United Kingdom, with the exception of Northern Ireland. There is still a struggle to provide the population with good jobs and good incomes. The economy still cannot create enough jobs to escape dependence upon imported jobs and substantial government subsidies.

The east of Wales, in the north and south, but not in the middle area, has experienced much faster economic growth and is more prosperous than the west. Cardiff, in particular, has grown impressively in economic terms, providing investment and financial services for many important British corporations.

The Enduring
English Connection

Even with devolution, the unequal relationship between less than 3 million Welsh and 47 million English must continue, with all of its ambiguous feelings and frequent stressful relationships. Over the centuries English cultural imperialism has been pervasive in Wales. Just as Welsh squires became anglicized in the days of Elizabeth I, Welsh workers have become anglicized through adhering to English political parties, trade unions, and popular culture, particularly as it appears in ubiquitous television programs.

Often Welsh resentment at English cultural imperialism comes to the surface. Parents complain that English television "brainwashes" their children. Country folk decry the English who buy cottages for the weekends or vacations and make the countryside less Welsh. These English purchasers have taken advantage of the cheaper properties in the rural settings that Wales has to offer. Sometimes when a Welsh person "puts on airs" he or she is sometimes admonished as "English." The Welsh reserve their greatest contempt for fellow Welsh who devote themselves to collaborating with English people perceived to be exploiting, patronizing or denigrating Welsh people.

Sometimes English newcomers in Wales outrage local citizens by not knowing traditional practices. For example, a new English owner might put a fence across his property and thereby cut a pathway that ran through it for centuries, a pathway that his neighbors had used since they were children.

A major complaint of Welsh people has been that most English people do not know much about Wales and do not bother to learn. English immigrants try to make their neighborhoods similar to those they left in England, just as if they settled in a remote part of the old British Empire. In school, whether in England or Wales, national history has meant English history. In fact, only a while ago, the notation for Wales in the *Encyclopedia Britannica* read: "For Wales, see England."

English newcomers tend to dislike the Welsh language. Almost invariably, they do not bother to learn any of it because they consider it an obscure anachronism. They find the pronunciations of place names horrendous and they worry that the Welsh have an advantage over them because they can communicate in privacy while they are present. English residents frequently complain when more hours of Welsh language television are programmed and when their children must learn Welsh in school.

Behind the relationship between the English and the Welsh is a long history of English attitudes of superiority that have been reflected in the pejoratives, or put-down terms, about Wales in the English language. To "welsh" out of something is to fail to pay a debt or fulfill an obligation. A "Welsh mile" is an interminable mile, and a fake object is sometimes said to be a "Welsh pearl." A "Welsh rabbit" turns out to be merely toasted cheese.

Welsh nationalists maintain that Wales is the oldest English colony. Undeniably, Wales has long been occupied by a more powerful neighbor possessing a larger economy, a powerful political system and a dominant language and culture. Over the centuries, countless English people have come to Wales to make their fortunes, just as others have done so in Canada or South Africa. On a lesser scale, many English in Wales make the imperialists' boast of owning the main businesses and having the Welsh work for them, as if they were an indigenous colonial people.

Nevertheless, there is ambivalence at the heart of the question of whether or not Wales has been a true colony of England. Even Welsh nationalists recognize that England has a magnificent tradition in law and politics, giving the whole world models for peaceful, workable constitutional government and effective jurisprudence. They recognize also that some of the greatest achievements of Welsh writers, poets and actors have been in the neighbor's language, which is, of course, the most widely used language in the world, and arguably the world's richest language.

Economic opportunity has been a two way street. Countless young and ambitious Welsh have made their fortunes in England, particularly in London or Liverpool. Countless others emigrated throughout the British Empire which, at its height, controlled over a quarter of the globe.

It can also be argued English domination of Wales has not been brutal. Indeed, many Irish nationalists would quickly agree to that proposition. But when rioters, such as Chartists or angry miners, rose against authority, British troops were quickly sent in to terminate disturbances. British garrison towns in Wales seemed to look like colonial outposts, displaying flags and sentries. Although the establishment of a bombing range activated

Welsh nationalism in the 1930's, British forces continue to use Wales to fire artillery, store ordinance and train troops. The celebrated anti-terrorist Special Air Service, or the SAS, is said to train in the Welsh mountains.

British imperialism anywhere always had its ambiguities. The British imperial mission was always a mixture of greed and benevolence. In Wales many English people did come to care about the principality, just as other English people in places like India came to care about Indian culture. Many English people appreciate Wales because much of contemporary Wales looks much like England did many years ago, what with its myriad of old Victorian terraced houses, fish and chip shops, cottages, small towns, churches with fair sized congregations and, overall, less affluence. English immigrants have also encountered a warm welcome from most Welsh people, whose hospitality rises to overcome whatever resentments various aspects of the colonial relationship have engendered.

The legacy of centuries of the relationship between the two nationalities has given rise to a variety of jokes and stereotypes, some of them quite hurtful. Beyond the stark images, however, is the realization that cultural norms are often different and that different emotional and social behaviors and styles are learned on each side of the border from childhood. In the worst circumstances, differences can lead to misunderstanding and negative stereotypes. In the best of circumstances, the two cultures can mutually enjoy each other's differences.

The most negative stereotypes of the Welsh depict them as country yokels who spout odd expressions such as "indeed to goodness." The Welsh are also characterized as dour Calvinists who are against good times and drink. Another stereotype puts them down as quick-witted talkers who are sly, shifty, devious and mercurial.

The Welsh costumes of the 19th century, largely invented for tourists, reinforce stereotypes. The stereotypical Welshman, Taffy, has a tall black hat and stockings, and the Welsh stereotypical woman appears in long skirts, shawls and tall black hats. In a later version, Taffy may appear in a cloth cap with coal stains on his face.

Negative stereotypes of the Welsh are counterbalanced by many positive ones. The Welsh are seen as so courteous that even the ferocious looking skinhead adolescents who are from Wales are reasonably polite. Welsh people are well known for their warm and genuine hospitality that excludes xenophobia. They are said to be the fastest people with the teapot and cake knife when visitors arrive. There is also an argumentative streak that brings forth contradictions quickly. The Welsh love Wales so much that they constantly write, sing, preach and discuss their homeland. Above all, the Welsh do not have the inhibitions and what they call the coldness of the English. This view links them to the Celts, who are supposed to be more romantic, temperamental and emotional than the cold English.

Many Welsh people all over Wales continue to have a sense of belonging to a greater community that is really like a very large extended family. They are usually engaged in the life of their community and practice much sociability that frequently includes the immense enjoyment of gossip. In this setting, they have a reputation for being easy going and sociable and perhaps inclined to procrastinate.

As small as Wales is, stereotypes have nevertheless developed among the Welsh themselves. They center on the differences between the northerners and the southerners. The southerners are seen as being so close to England and English inhabitants that they are said to have different accents, a more volatile temperament, and more sharpness. The northerners are depicted as more solemn and dour with their own more quiet sense of humor. In other words, they reflect the hard and remote environment of rural north Wales.

Social Changes in Contemporary Welsh Society

Social changes in Wales in recent decades have been massive, part of the impact of change that has cascaded over the United Kingdom and the rest of the developed world. Yet some developments had a stronger bearing upon Wales than upon the United Kingdom. A foremost example is the decline of religion, a European-wide phenomenon, of course, but one that was more keenly felt in Wales. Chapel congregations sharply declined after World War II as Wales and the rest of Europe became increasingly secular and materialistic. Chapels had been the key social institutions responsible for shaping the social mores and cultural expression of Wales. Chapels had taught ordinary Welsh people how to participate in democracy and how to administer an organization.

Recently crime rose alarmingly throughout the U.K., but Wales had always been known for having a comparatively low rate. So when south Wales became noted as the car theft center of Britain, many were astounded. In fact, statistics show that the largest police force in Wales, the South Wales Police, had a rate of notifiable offenses according to the population that was as high as the Metropolitan Police Force of London and the Merseyside Police Force of Liverpool.

Another important change involved gender roles. Besides the massive flow of women into the workforce of new industries, women's lives were dramatically changed by the widespread use of contraception. Modern Welsh women can plan pregnancy around their careers and employment. Other modern trends with a strong impact on Welsh women were the soaring rate of divorce and the decline of the nuclear family as the norm. Also, the percentage of births out of wedlock soared, although many such births reflected the replacement of marriage with some sort of partnership.

In general, both Welsh women and men have enjoyed a remarkable rise in standards of living in the last decades of the 20th century. Television sets, cars, telephones, washing machines and other durable goods have become the possessions of the mass of the population rather than just the privileged.

Many of the social changes had a decidedly positive effect on Welsh society. The National Health Service, dating from the late 1940's, raised the health standards of the whole principality. Until then, Wales had a reputation for poor health, including a high incidence of tuberculosis and other illnesses associated with poverty and deprivation. While the statistics for some diseases, such as cancer and heart disease, are still less favorable than for the rest of the United Kingdom, solid improvements in health care have profoundly changed the lives of most people in Wales. Moreover, increases in longevity and a fairly slow population rise have meant that the median age of the population has risen considerably.

Another positive change involves the large and growing number of young Welsh people who now enjoy higher education. Before World War II only a handful of youngsters could ever hope to go on to a university. By the 1970s, Wales had ten times the number of university students in comparison to the late 1930s. Yet only half of them are Welsh; English students make up most of the other half of the student population. On the other hand, half of the university students who are Welsh enroll in universities outside of Wales, which means England in most cases.

The tradition of valuing education remains strong in contemporary Wales. Many families have vivid memories of how education helped Welsh farmers' and miners' children join the middle class generations ago, very often as teachers or clergy. Today, education is relied upon to make Wales more modern and to strengthen the economy by preparing a skilled labor force for the new high-tech occupations.

Until recently the Welsh educational system was hard to distinguish from the English system, but now it is controlled from Wales and is tailored to Welsh interests. The use of Welsh in the schools, either for instruction or as a second language, exists with very few exceptions allowed. For primary school it is compulsory. Those favoring controversial bilingual education in the United States and elsewhere often look to Wales as a model.

Welsh children are required to start school at age 5 but an astounding 90 percent of three- and four year-olds participate in education on either a part time or full time basis. This may be in part a reflection upon the fact that modern Welsh families have mothers working away from the home.

A view of the modern campus of Swansea University.

With the influx of people of diverse background, some positive attitudinal changes have come about. A greater variety of lifestyles are tolerated to a degree that traditional Welsh society would not have accepted. Undoubtedly this increased acceptance has been in part due to the fact that increasing numbers of Welsh people can afford to travel to other parts of the United Kingdom, Europe and the world beyond.

The value of many post-war changes are matters of current debate: Supermarkets have disrupted the small town businesses clustered on high streets; poverty continues for many Welsh people in proximity to others who have enjoyed unprecedented recent affluence. The contrast

210

between the affluent and the poor has actually become starker than before.

Perhaps the most fundamentally debated change has been the inexorable dilution of the Welshness of Wales. The driving factor has been the migration of large numbers of English people and others to Wales, some to savor vacations, some to enjoy retirement and some to find affordable housing connected to commuter routes leading to their jobs in England. Meanwhile, young Welsh people have continued to seek better opportunities in England and overseas. As a result of these trends, the population in Wales has come to contain the lowest proportion of younger people and the highest proportion of retirement age people compared to any other part of the United Kingdom.

Increasingly, the traditional division in the Welshness of Wales between north and south has been replaced by a new division: The north has been replaced by the west as the bastion of Welsh culture, while the east has become the area of greatest English influence. Investment, prosperity and change have been strongest along two important motorways, the so-called M4 corridor in south Wales and the A55 expressway in north Wales.

As outsiders continue to move into the province, many new cultural divisions have developed in a variety of local areas. In particular, migration has been facilitated by the replacement of impoverished Welsh rural small holdings with large, mechanized farms. Consequently, countless buildings have become available for non-Welsh people who can afford them.

Unfortunately, many recent social changes in Wales are indisputably negative. Drug addiction has risen. The sense of community neighborliness has declined as a larger number of Welsh people live increasingly separate or atomistic lives, often preoccupied with television and computers in isolated housing developments. Community organizations, such as miners' social clubs and unions, have tended to fade away.

While the old image of Wales as a beautiful, mystical land of mountains, lakes and beaches continues, another quite grim Wales coexists with this idealized version. It is the Wales of rundown housing estates, often remote and isolated, where drug use, unemployment, single parenthood, car theft, property crime and various other social problems abound. Often these places are rubbish-strewn and rat-infested, lacking public facilities such as adequate bus service, telephones and post offices. People living in such environments are regarded as dangerous and are usually socially excluded from the rest of the population.

This grim Wales exists in patches, many of them in the west. Poverty in Wales is not absolute poverty, the kind that exists in many third world countries, where basic needs for food, clothing and shelter are not met. Wales has only relative poverty, meaning that a large number of people lack resources to maintain the lifestyle accepted as normal in a particular society. Measures to ameliorate this relative poverty are high on the agenda of the new Assembly of Wales.

The Continuing Struggle to Preserve Welsh Culture in the New Millennium

Evolving Welsh culture has survived the weak occupation of Rome, the onslaught of the Anglo-Saxons, the partial conquest of the Normans, the thorough conquest of the late Middle Ages, the amalgamation with England under the Tudors, the second-class status imposed for the language and everything else Welsh by the English, the massive changes from the Industrial Revolution, the emigration of the Welsh themselves, the influx of settlers from England and elsewhere, so-called mixed marriages, and the all-pervasive influence of Anglo-American television and films. Undoubtedly Welsh culture will survive in the new millennium.

Survival has often meant decline as well, and this is the case now. The Welshness of Wales continues to erode despite all the often frantic efforts of Welsh language enthusiasts as well as the carefully calculated and rather recent recognition of the value of the culture and language by the British government. Incidentally, some Welsh people suspect this new government appreciation is really an attempt to kill the culture with kindness.

Ask almost any ordinary American what image he has of Wales, and he or she is likely to respond by mentioning something about choral singing. Male and mixed voice choirs are still popular and still celebrated worldwide, but they are not as universal in Wales as before, thanks to the decline of the chapels and the rise of the entertainment industry. Choral singing by amateurs in the community could always draw the participation of poorest people and needed no rich patrons. By 1870 Wales was known as "the land of song," a cliché that has now become a popular inscription on tourist trade items.

As a result of the penchant to sing uninhibitedly at young ages, Wales has produced many famous singers who travel throughout the world today. The Welsh musical achievement is also manifested in a National Orchestra and a National Opera Company. In addition, Wales can claim some popular singers and some popular groups.

Wales is also a land of poets, artists, writers and actors, all of whom were helped in their early days by the Welsh tradition of amateur communal performance. One of the most famous poets of the 20th century was Dylan Thomas (1914–1953). He shuttled between Laugharne on the Welsh coast and London, broadcast on the BBC during World War II, went on lucrative lecture tours of the United States and, unfortunately, drank himself to death in New York. Richard Burton (1925–1984) was a powerful dramatic actor on stage and in films and the survivor of perhaps the most tempestuous Anglo-Welsh mixed marriage ever, that with Elizabeth Taylor.

Welsh sport is another source of Welsh cultural pride as well as a preoccupation that promotes national cohesiveness. Wales has a national rugby football team, and its games are very important events. Its star players become truly national heroes. It is said that nothing pleases the Welsh more than to have Englishmen suffer a defeat playing rugby in Wales. In football, or, as Americans say, soccer, Wales has four clubs, including one for Cardiff and one for Swansea. Other, more mildly popular sports, include cricket, a very English game; boxing, now in decline; and, rather recently, snooker, a pool hall game; and even darts has devoted adherents.

The Welsh love to celebrate St. David's Day, March 1, while the English are often not sure when their patron saint, St. George, has his special day. On St. David's Day Welsh daffodils are on exhibit; that peculiarly Welsh vegetable, the leek, is displayed; choruses sing that rousing nationalistic hymn, "Men of Harlech;" and big dinner celebrations and parties are held.

The real cultural apex for the Welsh is the Eisteddfod, held annually. It is an Olympic meet for poets, writers, and singers who use the Welsh language and it draws a crowd large enough to fill a football stadium. Prizes and awards are handed out. The Eisteddfod is reminiscent of an enormous Celtic tribal gathering and it is based upon the ancient gatherings of bards. Along with it goes some paraphernalia that some of the English find amusing, such as the use of swords, horns, crowns and wordy proclamations.

The Eisteddfod reaffirms and supports the Welsh cultural identity and does so in Welsh. Preserving the language and increasing its use is central to most Welsh nationalists. It remains an uphill struggle.

One consequence of non-Welsh migration to the northeast, southeast and throughout rural Wales is that there are no longer vast areas of the countryside where Welsh is spoken by most people. In other words, the old heartland of Welsh speakers has been fragmented. Now there are only many pockets where the ancient language predominates.

To counteract erosion of the language, the Welsh Language Society was launched in 1962. Many of its direct actions upset people who felt that a militant minority was seeking to impose its will upon the majority. They were seen as heroes by one side and fanatics by the other. They, and the language they fought for, were loved by some and loathed by others. Many are energetic young people eager to take action. They see their struggle for the language as another worthy struggle against the global push towards uniformity.

According to the 1991 census, just over half a million persons over three years old in Wales, or 18.6 percent of the population, could speak Welsh. This was down from 25 percent in 1970, 30 percent in 1950 and 40 percent in 1911. Although the ability to speak Welsh continues to erode, some striking recent developments have caused the rate of decline to slacken.

First of all, well-educated, middle-class, largely urban Welsh people in the most anglicized part of Wales, the populous southeast, particularly in and around Cardiff, have become ardent proponents of the language, insisting upon a greater use of Welsh in the school system. This pattern is similar to the push for Irish language education in Dublin by middle-class Irish nationalists with similar levels of education and attainment.

Both Welsh and Irish nationalists have been successful in bringing about Celtic language schools and bilingual programs in their respective countries. Throughout

Wales, some Welsh has become a requirement for primary schools and in the early stages of the secondary curriculum. While some schools use Welsh as the language of instruction, most teach Welsh as a second language. All of this has meant that there has been an increase in the number of Welsh speakers among younger people in the principality.

Many of the most ardent proponents of increased instruction in the Welsh language are graduates of the Welsh university system. Nevertheless, with so many English students at Welsh universities and so many Welsh students away at British universities, English has to continue to predominate in higher education.

A milestone in halting the rate of the erosion of the native tongue were the two previously mentioned Welsh Language Acts of 1967 and 1993. They decreed the equality of Welsh with English in public business and the administration of justice. These acts reversed the exclusive use of English that had been decreed by the Act of Union of 1536. Moreover, Welsh names for government bodies were acknowledged and government forms were also supplied in Welsh. Other bodies, such as companies, charities and credit unions, were required to include appropriate uses of Welsh. To reinforce these provisions, a Welsh Language Board was set up as a statutory body to promote the use of Welsh.

Further support for Welsh came from a government television channel that must use Welsh during peak viewing hours and a government radio station that uses Welsh exclusively at all hours. In addition, a number of programs to teach Welsh to adults were established and an increasing number of books have been published in the native language.

Not all of the recent developments have been positive for the ancient language. Just over half of the minority who speak Welsh regard it as their mother tongue rather than a second language. What is more, many Welsh people are best called semi-speakers, perhaps not unlike first or second generation Americans with European or Asian relatives. Also, many who claim to speak Welsh are unable to read or write the language effectively. Furthermore, the language may be degenerating in terms of grammar, as those who cannot speak it very well abandon more complicated and exacting forms of words. While this may simplify the language, it also makes it less flexible and less effective as a means of communication.

Another source of anxiety for Welsh speakers is devolution itself. Since institutions and increased governmental responsibility for Wales have emerged from devolution, this can be a sound new basis for Welsh nationalism instead of language. The new Welsh Assembly with its First Secretary will become increasingly important for Welsh identity. It should also be kept in mind that many important and famous Welsh in history were not Welsh speakers.

Before devolution, the Welsh nationality was strengthened by institutions that usually used English, such as the University of Wales, the National Library, National Museum, the Welsh Office and Secretary of State and national sports teams. Many ask whether a continuing struggle to sustain the Welsh language will be necessary in order to maintain Welsh nationalism after devolution.

Although it has become an act of modern political correctness for most politicians and non-speakers to continue to acknowledge the significance of the language, there are still those who regard it as a dying, difficult and impractical language which should be allowed to fade away quietly. This seems an unlikely prospect, but even if it does, there will always be a very special place called Wales.

Index